guide for

writers

www.thegoodwebguide.co.uk

thegoodwebguide for writers

Paul Chronnell

The Good Web Guide Limited • London

First Published in Great Britain in 2002 by The Good Web Guide Limited
65 Bromfelde Road, London, SW4 6PP
www.thegoodwebguide.co.uk

Email:feedback@thegoodwebguide.co.uk

© 2002 The Good Web Guide Ltd
Text © 2002 Paul Chronnell

Original series concept by Steve Bailey.

10 9 8 7 6 5 4 3 2 1

A catalogue record for this book is available from the British Library.

ISBN 1-903282-38-1

The publishers and author have done their best to ensure the accuracy and currency of all information in this volume, however they can accept no responsibility for any loss or inconvenience sustained by any reader as a result of its information or advice.

All rights reserved. No part of this publication may be reproduced, transmitted or stored in a retrieval system, in any form or by any means, except for the quotation of brief passages in reviews without permission in writing from The Good Web Guide Ltd.

Design by Myriad Creative Ltd

Printed in Italy at LEGO S.p.A.

contents

the good web guides	6
user key	9
acknowledgements	10
1 for sale	13
2 general	21
3 getting published	39
4 miscellaneous	53
5 non-fiction	61
6 prose	71
7 reference	83
8 screenwriting/playwriting	97
9 verse	119
glossary of internet terms	130
index	136

the good web guides

The World Wide Web is a vast resource, with millions of sites on every conceivable subject. There are people who have made it their mission to surf the net: cyber-communities have grown, and people have formed relationships and even married on the net.

However, the reality for most people is that they don't have the time or inclination to surf the net for hours on end. Busy people want to use the internet for quick access to information. You don't have to spend hours on the internet looking for answers to your questions and you don't have to be an accomplished net surfer or cyber wizard to get the most out of the web. It can be a quick and useful resource if you are looking for specific information.

The Good Web Guides have been published with this in mind. To give you a head start in your search, our researchers have looked at hundreds of sites and what you will find in the Good Web Guides is a collection of reviews of the best we've found.

The Good Web Guide recommendation is impartial and all the sites have been visited several times. Reviews are focused on the website and what it sets out to do, rather than an endorsement of a company, or their product. A small but beautiful site run by a one-man band may be rated higher than an ambitious but flawed site run by a mighty organisation.

Relevance to the UK-based visitor is also given a high premium: tantalising as it is to read about purchases you can make in California, because of delivery charges, import duties and controls it may not be as useful as a local site.

Our reviewers considered a number of questions when reviewing the sites, such as: How quickly do the sites and individual pages download? Can you move around the site easily and get back to where you started, and do the links work? Is the information up to date and accurate? And is the site pleasing to the eye and easy to read? More importantly, we also asked whether the site has something distinctive to offer, whether it be entertainment, inspiration or pure information. On the basis of the answers to these questions sites are given ratings out of five. As we aim only to include sites that we feel are of serious interest, there are very few low-rated sites.

Bear in mind that the collection of reviews you see here are just a snapshot of the sites at a particular time. The process of choosing and writing about sites is rather like painting the Forth Bridge: as each section appears complete, new sites are launched and others are modified. When you've registered at the Good Web Guide site (see p.159 for further details) you can check out the reviews of new sites and updates of existing ones, or even have them emailed to you.

As this is the first edition of the Good Web Guide, all our sites have been reviewed by the author and research team, but we'd like to know what you think. Contact us via the website or email feedback@thegoodwebguide.co.uk. You are welcome to recommend sites, quibble about the ratings, point out changes and inaccuracies or suggest new features to assess.

You can find us at
www.thegoodwebguide.co.uk

user key

£	subscription required
R	registration required
🔒	secure online ordering
UK / US	country of origin

acknowledgements

Writing may be an occasionally lonely process, but during the course of researching and writing this guide, I was lucky to have the help and support of a number of wonderful people. In different ways, some large, some small, they all helped me make this book happen.

Becca, Dreyfuss and Eddie. Thank you for all that patience, those mountains of optimism when I desperately needed to hear it and those tumble-weed filled, 'for my own good', silences when I was horrid.

As ever, I have to thank my parents who never fail to surprise me with the extent of their encouragement and support.

Ongoing thanks must be loaded onto the shoulders of Miles, for always managing to be interested, sharing my sense of humour and my understanding that an hour in a busy day is not a long time, but friends can always find time to squeeze in a couple of pints and some quality chat.

Thanks also to Claire, for guarding my back up disc with her life; Lucy for looking after the cats and not breaking my computer; and all the guys from The Palace Theatre who realise that 'When I get free, you won't see me here for dust' is not just a line from a play, but a promise to ourselves.

Warm thanks also to Elaine and all those at The Good Web Guide for thinking this guide was a good idea and for being quietly confident that I'd deliver on time.

Finally, huge thanks go to all the site owners who offered encouragement, congratulations and answered my questions. I know the readers of this guide will be in good hands.

Ta very much to you all.

Chapter 01
for sale

Oh, the notion of a writer is a wonderful thing. Sitting in a dingy garret room, struggling with a blank piece of paper, shunning family and friends while sweating each individual word. And all the while, struggling with a powerful muse who seems to be absent more often than not. Romantic? Stupid, more like.

No one will think your writing is any better just because the process nearly destroyed or reduced you to tears. Get all the help you can. Absolutely. The following sites offer writing software to make the whole creative process easier. There are entire shops dedicated to writers, and remember, a decent writing book is wonderful for whacking your muse around the head with. She'll soon start toeing the line.

Obviously, as this is a 'for sale' chapter, you will be parting with cash to get these products, so shop around, search the internet, and make sure you're getting the best value for your money.

www.scriptsales.com
Done Deal

Overall rating: ★★★★		
Classification: Guide	**Content:**	★★★★★
Updating: Sporadically	**Readability:**	★★★★★
Navigation: ★★★★★	**Speed:**	★★★★★

US

It is very unusual, if not unheard of, for a site to have two entries in a Good Web Guide. However, in this instance, it is warranted, because the sections of Done Deal concerned with buying products are absolutely excellent and a must for anyone planning to part with their money, and as this chapter only deals with buying products, we didn't want you to miss it in the other Done Deal review. The only two sections we will concern ourselves here are under the Advice and Feedback section of the homepage.

SPECIAL FEATURES

Angle On If you are planning to invest in some writing software, you will have noticed that it does not come cheap. You will also have noticed that the homepages of the various products make their software sound like the only viable option, buy any other at your peril. What is needed is independent thinking on what's available, and that's exactly what you get here. Eleven products are reviewed. All have a ratings system, so various attributes can be compared. All the reviews are intelligent and comprehensive. Of course, these are only one person's opinions, but they help you get started. You'll be glad you read these reviews before ordering any of the featured products.

Bookshelf Thirty books receive the same in depth reviewing as the software did. Again, different aspects of the books

are rated. The only thing you'll need to do is ignore the purchasing advice and look for the titles on UK based book selling sites. We recommend www.amazon.co.uk.

When self-help materials are so expensive, reviews like these could save you a small fortune.

www.finaldraft.com
Final Draft

Overall rating: ★ ★ ★ ★			
Classification:	E-commerce	Content:	★ ★ ★ ★
Updating:	Weekly	Readability:	★ ★ ★ ★ ★
Navigation:	★ ★ ★ ★ ★	Speed:	★ ★ ★ ★ ★
US			

Final Draft claim to be the world's best selling screenwriting program, unless of course, you talk to the makers of Scriptware (see review in this chapter). Virtually every site dedicated to the art of screenwriting will mention Final Draft. It is fully endorsed by Oliver Stone, Tom Hanks, James L. Brooks (As Good As It Gets) and Michael Bay (Pearl Harbour). But what is it? Well, essentially, it's a specially put together word processor, especially designed to take all the hassle out of formatting scripts. This means instead of worrying about margins or spacing or scene headings you can concentrate on more important things, like plot, characters, suspense and writing an Oscar winning screenplay. It's not cheap, especially if you order it from America, so if you're going to buy, find it in Britain first. This site recommends UK customers should purchase it from www.thescreenwritersstore.co.uk which is reviewed elsewhere in this chapter. This site has a fresh, modern look and is navigated using the links on the left of each and every page.

SPECIAL FEATURES

Products Find out exactly what you're getting for your money. The first four links under this heading take you to specific pages dedicated to different products. Essentially these are just different versions of Final Draft. Read the product information to find the one that suits you best. There are also some demos which you can download for free. The information is concise but clear, and is, of course, predominantly aimed at getting you to part with your cash. They recommend Syd Field's video workshop here too.

Support Centre Before you buy, why not download a demo version of the product you're interested in. If you do buy, you can also feel fairly safe that any problems you encounter will be covered here in the fairly comprehensive Online Knowledge Base.

Writers Resources There's a newsletter which is free. After typing in your name and email address, choose Subscribe from the drop down menu and you'll be added to the mailing list. You can find details of a script registering service which is an advert for another site that provides the service. There are a number of forums for a range of discussion topics. You'll also find some useful links to other sites.

Press Centre News, Reviews and more than a few people, some very famous, offer more glowing reports about using the software.

If you want to make the mechanics of scriptwriting easier, and you have the money to spare, this site will show you how.

www.masterfreelancer.com
Master Freelancer

Overall rating: ★★★★			
Classification:	E-commerce	Content:	★★★★★
Updating:	Weekly	Readability:	★★★★★
Navigation:	★★★★★	Speed:	★★★★★

(US)

From a British point of view, it is a shame that most of the excellent sites like this, selling you writing software, books and other self-help items are based in America. This means the pricing is in dollars, there is a much greater delivery charge and a much longer wait until your purchase arrives at your door. Some sites won't even deliver outside of the US.

This site will deliver all over the world, but all the other problems above are still relevant. However, there is such a good selection of products here, that it is still worthy of inclusion in this guide. There are specialised categories for Screenwriters, E-Books for Writers, Audio Tapes and Life Writing (to help you write your own life story or write a journal). With all of these products, we suggest you search for them in UK online stores for your purchasing convenience.

The site has a clear, sharp design, the pages load quickly and navigation is easy. Choose from the tabs at the top of the page, or the colourful icons down the left of the page, to take you where you want to go.

SPECIAL FEATURES

Writing Software Create plots, build stories, find markets, lay out your manuscript and more. Software titles can be clicked for a full page describing the main features. Items are delivered on CD or floppy disk. Some have demo versions you can download.

Screenwriting Software All the industry leaders, plus software to help you make a movie, find contacts, organise yourself and your thoughts, and sample contracts.

E-Book Store Self-help writing guides that will be sent to you as e-mails within 24 hours. Almost all the books require the Adobe Acrobat Reader, which you can download here for free. If you don't currently have the reader, download it now, even if you're not planning on buying a book. You never know when you'll need it.

Books At the time of writing, this section contained 111 books in 17 categories. Each title has a brief summary of the book contents. A further click will bring up a page dedicated to that book alone, with more detailed information.

Creative Pros' Newsstand Loads of magazines, newsletters and business related titles. Filled with American content, but most can be shipped to you anywhere in the world.

Audio / Video Selection of titles variously available on audio cassette, video or CD. Novel way of honing your writing skills.

Life Writing Titles to help you with your personal journal and writing from your experiences. Includes software and books.

Other Features There are books listing the current pricing rates and market guides for freelance work. Much of the pricing content is too Americanised to be of use to UK writers. The New Products section lists, not surprisingly, the newest site additions. These new products are also available from their relevant sections of the site. In Best Buys, you'll find all the major money saving bargains. There are also Writer's Resources which include a free newsletter, author interviews, and if you're interested, you can also get a free email account. There are also a good assortment of free software downloads, but be warned, some of them are huge and will take quite some time to download..

Excellent variety of products to help you write more successfully and efficiently.

www.screenwriterstore.co.uk
Screenwriters Store

Overall rating: ★ ★ ★ ★			
Classification:	E-commerce	Content:	★ ★ ★ ★ ★
Updating:	Weekly	Readability:	★ ★ ★ ★ ★
Navigation:	★ ★ ★ ★ ★	Speed:	★ ★ ★ ★ ★

UK

Originally based right in the heart of Soho, London but now moved to the south east of the city, the Screenwriters Store proclaims itself to be Europe's 'largest authorised reseller and distributor of Screenwriting and Production software'. And why would they lie? This is a one stop shop for all your screenwriting needs, so you needn't worry about trying anywhere else first. The site has a light touch and chatty writing tone. You really feel at ease here and feel secure that you are seeing all the products in their best possible light. The latest and favourite products fill the homepage, whilst all further products are available from the links at the very top of the page. Their products include software packages, cassettes, magazines and books. Add to this regular film news, and a variety of articles about screenwriting and you'll find yourself coming back again and again.

SPECIAL FEATURES

Products The bread and butter of the site. Products are categorised according to use. There are sections for Formatting, Story Development, Film Making and related software, Books and Mags, as well as General Software Products, which currently has only one piece of software, that allows you to dictate your screenplay, which is an interesting idea. All products can be paid for using a secure server, so you don't have to worry about giving your credit card details.

News Events, updates and new product releases. This is also where you'll find related articles.

Downloads Lots and lots of scripts to download for free. Some can be downloaded immediately, others will be sent to you via email. All the necessary details are laid out very simply for each title. You may require the free Adobe Acrobat Reader, and there's a link for those of you who don't have it.

FAQS All the frequently asked questions for various products, mostly Final Draft. Soon there will also be a list of UK agents willing to look at unsolicited manuscripts without charging a reading fee. Very useful indeed.

Competition Every month, answer the question for the chance to win screenwriting related prizes. Recent prizes have included magazine subscripts and a copy of Final Draft, which can't be bad.

Links Important places, especially for UK writers. Go check them out.

Courses and Tuition Includes 'in the flesh' seminars as well as courses on CD.

Friendly site, great products useful articles. You write screenplays and they sell stuff to make the process easier.

http://scriptware.com/			
Scriptware			
Overall rating: ★★★★			
Classification:	E-commerce	Content:	★★★
Updating:	Occasionally	Readability:	★★★
Navigation:	★★★★★	Speed:	★★★★★
US			

Simply put, Scriptware formats your screenplay while you type, so you don't lose the creative flow. Just like the Final Draft site (reviewed earlier in this chapter), it claims to be the worlds best-selling software for screenplay writers. They can't both be, but who knows who's right? However, these two definitely seem to be the industry leaders. This site is more flashy than it's competitor. Lots of areas of the front page literally flash to get your attention, which works but maybe becomes a little bit irritating after a while. There is a compelling review for the software, which is linked to the opening page as 'Click here for Done Deal's Scriptware version 3 review'. They seem to like it. Many of the site features have one word links to other pages in the body of the homepage information. But, so you don't miss anything, it's better to go to the links at the bottom of this and every subsequent page. Is it better than Final Draft? You'll have to download both free demos, one from each official site and decide for yourself.

SPECIAL FEATURES

Features As you would expect, here is where the capabilities of the program are laid bare for your approval. Equally expected is that everything is a plus point and nothing negative. However, it does have some pretty impressive features and everything is described in a simple, user-friendly way. You could say it worries about the more boring necessities of scriptwriting while you throw yourself into the far more interesting writing part.

See It Very useful section where you can see actual screen grabs of the programme at work. They are presented as a user controlled slideshow and the short descriptions that go with the slides will further whet your appetite for this product.

It's Easy A sample page of script, with notes about how Scriptware would make the whole writing process easier for you, if only you had it.

Q & A All your queries and worries are dealt with. Every single one of them is an incentive to buy the software.

Guest Registry If you want to download the demo or just want to be kept up to date with products and services that help you write, then fill out this form.

Links If you can cope with even more screenwriting sites, there are lots more here to ensure you never leave the house again.

Ordering If you're not in America, click the Dealers link to find UK and other supplies around the world. Our advice is to try The Screenwriter's Store, reviewed elsewhere in this chapter.

Makes screenwriting easier, which can only be a good thing, but like most writing software it's expensive, so make sure you try out the demo before you buy.

www.sophocles.net
Sophocles

Overall rating: ★★★★★		
Classification: E-commerce	Content:	★★★★★
Updating: Monthly	Readability:	★★★★★
Navigation: ★★★★★	Speed:	★★★★★

(US)

Just another piece of screenwriting software? Well, the people at Sophocles are very keen to point out that their product is different from its rivals. With Sophocles, the emphasis is on the Writing Process, actually helping you create a story, as well as making sure it's set out properly on the page. Aimed at creativity rather than formatting. The site carries the usual list of recommendations from a small group of industry professionals. These are towards the bottom of the homepage. Don't worry if the example screenshots throughout the site look a little fuzzy on your computer. A single click will enlarge the shot until it fills your screen, giving you extremely clear pictures of what the programme looks like in all its glory. The navigation bar is at both the top and bottom of the page, which couldn't be simpler.

SPECIAL FEATURES

Features Four full pages of features, including thirteen full screenshots. As you work your way through, you have to agree that this sounds like an excellent purchase for any creative screenwriter.

Download As with all these large, generally expensive pieces of software, there is a free download to make your mouth water before you even think about buying. There is a very useful step by step guide to make the process extremely simple. Apart from one or two features, the trial version is the same as the registered version. To unlock the entire programme you will need to register and then part with $160 (US). What this means is that there is no CD or hard copy version of the programme. You download the whole thing off the internet, and that's that.

Register Easy to follow instructions and a useful Frequently Asked Registration Questions page, which will help to clear up any confusions or worries you might have.

Support Need a little help? Want to suggest something? Got another sort of question? This is where to come.

Another informative site with a more creative take on screenwriting software.

www.writersstore.com
The Writers Store

Overall rating: ★★★		
Classification: E-commerce	Content:	★★★★
Updating: Daily	Readability:	★★★★★
Navigation: ★★★★★	Speed:	★★★★

US

With twenty years experience selling products to writers, this Los Angeles based company have a helpful, informative, well designed site, stacked full of useful products. As well as writing and screenwriting, check out the products for selling your script and genre-specific items about romance or crime writing. Those of you who want to write and make your own films will not be disappointed by the Film Making category. The Writers Store will supply their wares anywhere in the world and already have chalked up 100,000 customers. So you can rest assured they obviously have a pretty fair idea about what they're doing. The three main site links are grey tabs at the top of this first page. More specifically, the Most Popular Categories are a little further down the page, and for a complete overview you can view all categories using the link at the top left of the page under the Browse Categories heading, which is very helpful if the main pages aren't quite specific enough for you.

SPECIAL FEATURES

Script Writing The most popular of all writing purchases. Although the site don't want to come down in favour of a particular product, they do list the top sellers down the left of the page. The page is conveniently arranged for easy access to nearly fifty Software titles; more than three hundred books; Supplies, but if you can't find these in your local stationary shop you're simply not looking hard enough; several dozen Audio titles and there are even Workshops and Seminars. For additional savings try the bundled packages.

Creative Writing Software More software, more descriptions, more downloads and more FAQs. The details are free but the full products all cost rather a lot of money. They all cost rather a lot too.

Creative Writing Writing for anything other than the screen? This is the place for you. The page format is the same as above, with books, software, supplies, etc., all set out in an extremely user friendly fashion.

Film making Includes more software for those who want to actually make films. These promise to help with scheduling and budgeting and other similar problems.

Other Features There's a very useful search feature at the top of the page, and don't forget to sign up for the free ezine which features items about screen and creative writing.

Loads of choice, especially books. Everyone needs help sometimes and this site offers products with loads of it.

Chapter 02
general

If your writing doesn't fit nicely into one of the other chapter headings in this guide, or if you are new to the whole writing game, the following sites are where you want to start browsing. They are here for a number of reasons. Some of the sites are so big and cover so many genres, they don't fit anywhere more specific. Some are writing communities who welcome everyone with open arms, no matter what your speciality.

Don't think for a minute that because the chapter is 'general' the sites provide non-specific content. They are all as focused as any other websites. They have fantastic content. They know what they're talking about. They will help your writing. You will improve, of that there is no doubt.

Fiction, Non-fiction, Poetry, Scripts, The Business, Selling your work, all these areas are covered, often on the same site. Many of the sites share similarities, but some will appeal to you more than others. Check them all out and see which you are drawn to.

www.absolutewrite.com
Absolute Write

Overall rating: ★★★★		
Classification: Guide	**Content:**	★★★★★
Updating: Weekly	**Readability:**	★★★★★
Navigation: ★★★★★	**Speed:**	★★★★★

US

A site with a sense of humour. And not a 'wahay, aren't we wacky' kind of humour, more a witty, light hearted, 'we enjoy what we do' humour. Which immediately endears you to it. It's a little overwhelming at first in that it's difficult to know where to go. A little browsing is in order first. Eventually the conclusion will be reached that there is a wealth of articles columns, links, markets and reviews all aimed at making your writing better and then giving yourself the best possible chance of selling it.

If you are currently putting words together, trying to get them in the best order and maybe hoping someone will buy the finished product off you, then you need the links on the Take Me To line. Everyone else can amuse themselves with the links next to the green dots just underneath the site title.

SPECIAL FEATURES

Play/Screenwriting Lots of good articles. Then there is even more to be learnt from industry professionals who share some thoughts. There are also regular columns, links, latest news and a fairly lively message board. This is pretty much a screenwriting site all on it's own.

Freelance Writing More of the same for those writers writing articles. There is also a huge list of markets and freelance news items of the moment.

Novels & Non-Fiction News, articles, interviews, and reviews of relevant books.

Speciality Writing A little something for writers who specialise in e-books, poetry, short stories, technical writing, comic books, newsletters, books for children and even one-liners.

E-Zines Want information sent to your computer without the need to do anything other than give your email address? You know you do. Seven such lists that all come highly recommended. They include a screenwriting list, an erotica writing list and a variety of newsletter filled with general news, tips and articles.

Fun Stuff When you can't bear to write another word amuse yourself for hours with these links to things to make you laugh.

Other Features Absolute Write will design your website for you, for a fee, obviously. You can also buy books, software and merchandise but it's all in dollars and in America, so if anything takes your fancy, search for it on British sites. There are also even more market links listed.

Large site that takes on a lot of genres and succeeds at them all.

www.author.co.uk
Author.co.uk

Overall rating: ★★★★★		
Classification: Community	**Content:**	★★★★★
Updating: Constantly	**Readability:**	★★★★★
Navigation: ★★★★★	**Speed:**	★★★★★

UK

Nearly a thousand pages, and over a million words of help and advice for writers. Phew. This British site has collected articles, stories, news, reviews and more. It even has a growing section where British Authors and their books are promoted. So that you are not bogged down with text, each section begins with a sort of homepage of its own, where the features are succinctly described so you can quickly decide if you are interested in what's on offer. If you are, simply click the word or words highlighted in blue and you're taken to the full story. It's nicely designed and all the pages are crisp and clear and load quickly. The main page is taken up with a selection of links to the more recent writing news from around the web. In the not too distant future the whole guide will be available on a CD for offline viewing. They are also planning to soon be linked to a whole range of online courses. So the future looks roses.

The main links for the site are on the left hand side of the main page and are accessible from every page you go to after that.

SPECIAL FEATURES

Authors At the time of writing, almost 150 British Authors have their own homepages at Author.co.uk . It costs as little as £40 to have a page of your own. Writers have used these pages to promote their already published works, or simply to promote themselves and their writing skills. What you use it for is very much up to you. Find out how to get one by clicking the **services** link.

Contacts Simply excellent, well organised and crystal clear. Loads of links for magazines, publishers, children's writing, readers, reviewers, audio books, literary and university sites and an excellent list of sites that publish ebooks.

Ebooks Learn what exactly they are, how they work, the pitfalls involved and more.

Magazine Articles, interviews, book reviews, even a crossword.

Services Through the site you can get help with document presentation, publishing ebooks and details of how to set up your own website.

Writing A growing section to help you write by sparking ideas, gently getting the creative juices flowing and discussing a broad selection of writing topics. If you can think of anything to add to this section, they're more than happy to hear from you.

OTHER FEATURES

Circles Growing all the time, this page features writer's circles, organised geographically so you can find one near you with ease. This is not a comprehensive list of circles, instead, each group has actively chosen to have it's details represented here.

Ezine Arrives fortnightly and it's free. Keep in touch with what's going on at the site.

News Loads and loads about the recent goings on in the world of writing.

Clear, concise, helpful and encouraging to all writers, with even more to come.

www.blackonwhite.on.ca		
Black on White		
Overall rating: ★★★★★		
Classification: Guide	**Content:**	★★★★★
Updating: Monthly	**Readability:**	★★★★★
Navigation: ★★★	**Speed:**	★★★★★
CAN		

Any site that describes itself as 'a place where writers can come together just when you feel like throwing up all over your keyboard', absolutely has to be worth a look. Click the typewriter to enter the site proper. Once there, you are faced with the site's mission statement. The angle they've taken is that they want to help writers overcome the blocks that stop them putting words down on paper. Interesting this also includes 'Fear', that can stop you working. And you'll be happy to know that the site is for all writing minded people, nothing particular is required to get involved, and it won't cost you a penny.

It's a pleasant looking site which reads clearly and loads quickly, (two of our favourite website attributes). It also has a nice sense of humour throughout which is worth even more brownie points. Currently there are more than 900 members of the site.

Most, but not all, the site links are available by clicking Table of Contents at the bottom of the opening page. However, for a list of everything the site offers, click the links on the left of the page, on the piece of paper coming out of the typewriter. You'll notice that the Table of Contents and the links on the left often have different titles. Which is mildly irritating.

SPECIAL FEATURES

The Dust Jacket All writers know this, but it's still a relief to hear Scott, the original writer behind the site, spell out how easy it is to find reasons not to write. He has an amusing, chatty tone which immediately puts you at ease. You just know he's making perfect sense.

The Prefix This is where you find out what you should be doing before you spill out a single word onto your blank page. It's about planning. It covers Character, Plot, Theme and Setting. And it's a really useful way to get your project moving, rather than simply staring at the walls.

Non-fiction Help An interesting article by Tim Philp, a non-fiction writer who scratches the shine off the industry by admitting that he hates writing, finds it really difficult and explains how marketing is more important than talent.

New Contracts Sign a contract with yourself to get a project finished. Your promise is then sent to the mailing list who will encourage you to complete your work and honour that contract. When you have made progress, fill in the Contract Updates page and let everyone else know how you're doing.

Other Features A FAQ page answers the burning questions of the site as well as 'How do I make a good Harvey Wallbanger?' and the equally important 'Why is the Sky Blue?' The Fair Play section outlines how to be fair to yourself and others as you spend time at the site and on the mailing list. Petri Dish is a short article offering, by example, how you can purge your life of the paper clutter that constantly builds up. Publishing Help offers advice for when you have managed to get something finished and are wondering how to take it to the next stage. The Mailing List has more than 300 members and is a busy forum for discussion. There are also the usual collection of useful links to other site.

Great site. Doesn't promise anything, other than to get your writing moving, which is sometimes more than half the battle.

www.coffeehouseforwriters.com
Coffeehouse for Writers

Overall rating: ★ ★ ★ ★ ★			
Classification:	Community/Commerce	**Content:**	★ ★ ★ ★
Updating:	Regularly	**Readability:**	★ ★ ★ ★ ★
Navigation:	★ ★ ★ ★ ★	**Speed:**	★ ★ ★ ★ ★
US			

This is a writing community, combined with a useful online business providing courses and workshops for writers. The first thing to greet you is a funky Flash intro which is well worth watching. It has a feel a little like the American comedy Friends. Maybe this is just what you need to get you in the writing mood first thing on an otherwise dull morning. The site is neither too busy or too boring and the tone and atmosphere are friendly and welcoming.

The opening page has the latest site news but to really get around, click the tabs at the top of the homepage.

SPECIAL FEATURES

Make Friends All the links in this section run down the left of the page, with some tasters in the main column of the page. Here you'll find a variety of email lists, including The Poetry Café; Coffeehouse Buzz where you can brag about your successes; WriterSwap Knowledge Exchange where writers swap advice and expertise to help with research for projects; Coffeehouse Writing Perc for brewing fresh ideas; and Coffeehouse Percolator where members offer helpful feedback on each other's work. Find out more about these last two lists in the Get Motivated section of the site.

Also in this section are personal classified ads and writers looking to make new friends with other writers.

While you're here, why not sign up for both the free newsletters filled with advice about writing and being a writer.

Learn the Craft Lots of online writing workshops, covering all areas of the writing process. They involve students who have access to a private message board and a tutor online. Assignments are set and critiqued, like any other writing course, but these you can do at home, when it suits you, and, as is suggested, in your pyjamas and slippers if you like. They all cost you money, many are in the region of $75, some are considerably more. Payment is via a PayPal account, which you will have to set up first.

Writing Tips Helpful articles and, not unsurprisingly, tips for writers.

Other Features There are lists of current competitions and a very useful Grammar Test.

Overall, this is a great place to meet other writers, make friends and improve your skills.

http://ewritelife.com/
eWriteLife

Overall rating: ★★★★★			
Classification:	Guide	**Content:**	★★★★★
Updating:	Monthly	**Readability:**	★★★★★
Navigation:	★★★★★	**Speed:**	★★★★★

(SI)

It wouldn't be true to say this site was a unique experience, that it provided a forum and a community that cannot be found anywhere else on the internet. It has many of the same features, albeit, with different content, that quite a few other writing sites have. There are articles, advice, shopping, research links and everything you will come to expect from writing guides like this. However, although similar, all these writing sites have very distinct flavours. No two are exactly the same. Some you will find suitable, others less so. This site will appeal to those writers who don't want to feel threatened by the hard sell of writing. This site is about achieving at your own pace in a friendly environment rather than a 'How to make a million in your first weekend as a writer' kind of site. This site is as attractive to look at as it is useful to delve into to. The site links are available across the top of the homepage or in the blue column running down the right. This site is still growing and has not yet reached the 'established' web site status. But word will get round about this funky site. It's too good to miss

SPECIAL FEATURES

Articles Fiction, Non-fiction, Markets, Interviews. All the articles are a pleasant ramble, picking up wonderful tips along the way. Relaxed, yet extremely rewarding.

Columns Regular columns by individual columnists reside here. It's early days and these sections are going to grow and grow.

Exercises Need a kick-start? Maybe you don't have time to work on a lengthy piece of writing, but want to keep your hand in? You're in the right place. The QuickWrite section will have you racing off some words in no time. Anyone who is inspired to complete any of the exercises here in the Writing Gym is invited to send it in for everyone to read. Again, these sections are growing steadily, so get involved now.

Tools Free and complete ebooks for you to download. Freeware/Shareware programmes for writers. They include a very useful manuscript management programme for you to keep track of your submissions. There is also a small selection of recommended writing links.

Workshops If you fancy a rather more hands on approach to improving your writing, you may well find it here. A good selection of online workshops at fairly reasonable prices.

Community Lots of message boards on a variety of topics, but they are rather slow moving at the moment. Get in there, get writing, you only get out what you put in.

This is a great site. When word spreads, it's sure to establish itself as an essential site for writers.

www.manistee.com/~lkraus/workshop/index.html				
Internet Writing Workshop				
Overall rating: ★ ★ ★ ★				
Classification:	Workshop		**Content:**	★ ★ ★ ★
Updating:	Constantly		**Readability:**	★ ★ ★
Navigation:	★ ★ ★ ★ ★		**Speed:**	★ ★ ★ ★ ★
US				

Sometimes you want to get someone else to have a look at your work and to have them offer some constructive criticism. Someone perhaps who isn't so close to you that their opinion is biased. Oddly enough, that's exactly what goes on here. They are an online workshop. You write a piece of work, then send it to this list and other writers will give you valuable feedback on it. Before you send in your first piece, you are required to write a critique for someone else's work, which is only fair. Check out the Frequently Asked Questions for all the rules.

This is a large site, with several genres of writing having their own workshops. Everyone is required to join the general Writing List and at least one other from Screenwriting, Novels, Young Adults, Love Stories, Teen, Basic Practice, Flash Fiction, and Poetry workshops too. Something for everyone.

It's free to join and the only membership criteria is that you participate in the lists you have joined. There's no real site as such, except for a page giving the basic information about what happens here, all the workshop activity is via email. Towards the bottom of the page you will find links to all the different parts of the site. Some of the page backgrounds are a little busy, which can make them hard to read sometimes, but that doesn't stop the information loading fairly quickly.

SPECIAL FEATURES

Frequently Asked Questions Not so much of a feature, as a necessity. A lot of writers have been active on these lists for some time, so make sure you understand exactly how it all works, and what's expected of you when you join. These FAQs couldn't be much clearer. Ignore them at your peril.

Nonfiction This workshop is mentioned as a special feature simply because it fairly unusual for non-fiction writers to have this sort of outlet for their work on the internet. See separate entry in the Non-fiction chapter of this guide.

How-to Books suggestions If you would still rather buy yourself some help rather than find it for free on the internet, this section lists dozens of books, with information on every aspect of writing and its pitfalls.

To get the most out of this site you need to participate. You won't be sorry that you did.

www.thescriptorium.net		
The Scriptorium		
Overall rating: ★★★★		
Classification: Webzine	Content:	★★★★★
Updating: Monthly	Readability:	★★★★★
Navigation: ★★★★★	Speed:	★★★★
CAN		

Wonderful looking site that has obviously had as much time spent on how it looks as what it contains. Little chance of eye-strain here, no matter how many hours are spent pouring over the content, and there could be many. The whole site is basically a monthly ezine, containing lots of helpful, advice filled, articles for every sort of writer. The homepage contains snippets and then links to all the new stuff, while the icons across the top of the page will take you to all the relevant articles of that section. But first things first, go to the darker left hand column, put your name where it says Name and your email address where it says Email. Now you're signed up on the mailing list for either the newsletter or, if you prefer, updates only. You choose, it's completely free.

SPECIAL FEATURES

On Writing This month's offering of articles for both fiction and non-fiction writers. At the time of writing the current topics under discussion included the importance of good titles, writing quickly, writing elegantly and revealing character.

Creativity Get your writing moving with these excellent 'freewriting' exercises and monthly set homework.

Toolbox Includes a form for others, as well as yourself, to critique your work; a form to keep track of your submissions; two forms for getting to know your characters; and a wonderful feature, which at the time of writing, isn't quite ready, but will be very soon, called World Builder which will help you build realistic settings for your writing.

Software Concise reviews and links of downloadable software from other sites. Some of it is even free. Check the size of the programs before you start to download, some of them are quite big. The programmes that cost money are all priced in US dollars.

Young Writers This site within a site is a wonderful resource for the younger writers out there. Without the slightest hint of patronisation the site offers articles, resources, recommended books, exercises and even some writing by young writers.

Archives Surprisingly small selection of archived articles, but we are assured that many more are on the way soon. The excellent exercises, however, seem to go on forever, which is a huge plus. There are more book reviews too.

Other Features The Reading section has book reviews and links to Amazon.com to buy them. Articles has expert comment and essays on any and all aspects of writing. There are lots and lots of categorised links with brief but extremely useful descriptions.

Elegant site, great content, especially good for kick starting creativity.

http://welcome.to/Wordweave			
Wordweave			
Overall rating: ★★★★			
Classification:	Community	**Content:**	★★★★★
Updating:	Monthly	**Readability:**	★★★★★
Navigation:	★★★★★	**Speed:**	★★★★★
UK US			

A very helpful homepage reads a little like one of the reviews in this Good Web Guide. Each section is taken in turn and a brief description leaves you in doubt of what to expect when you arrive there. Basically, this excellent site has articles, a newsletter, a message board, creative activities and very reasonably priced workshops (in US dollars). It's the sort of site you can simply drop into for a moment, read some comment, grab some tips, or sit down, park your coffee mug and spend the rest of the day here. The unfussy design makes for pleasant surfing and the pages load fast into your browser. The links for navigating the site are on the right hand side and remain there as you wander from place to place.

SPECIAL FEATURES

Activities Fantastic list of creativity starters. What makes this selection so good, is that they're fun to do so don't feel like homework or worse. Currently there are more than 90 exercises for you to try. Once you've tackled a few, you're sure to be able to continue in the same vein and make some up of your own.

Workshop Wordweave workshops run at different times of the year and are fee to participate in. There are also lots of links to Inspired2write.com workshops, which are very reasonable in price, usually have a membership limit of 15 people and take place as a private email group. Each workshop group has an instructor who guides the participants through a number of prearranged and easy to follow stages. Sign up for the free newsletter to hear about new workshops first.

Writings Themes are set, writers are inspired to create something in the mood of the theme, then pages are designed to display the results. Great writing on the whole. Feel free to be equally inspired and get involved.

Archive If you're looking for an article, there are dozens. They cover a huge range of topics. The only downside is that they are not in any sort of order, so you have to try and guess what the articles contain, from only the title. A little categorisation might be useful. Wordweave assure us that this small problem will be addressed in the not too distant future.

Here you will also find all the past issues of the monthly newsletter going back to May 1999.

Newsletter The current edition and details of how to subscribe, which is also available from the Subscribe link in the main list.

Write Now! Fairly busy message board where writers request feedback on their own writing, meet other writers, promote themselves and their sites or simply ask for help with writing problems. In order to post to the board you have to log in. Click the Login link to create your free account.

Excellent site to get you started, keep you going, guide you along the way, whilst all the time making sure it's an enjoyable ride.

www.writers-exchange.com
Writers Exchange

Overall rating: ★ ★ ★ ★		
Classification: Guide	Content:	★ ★ ★ ★ ★
Updating: Frequently	Readability:	★ ★ ★
Navigation: ★ ★ ★ ★	Speed:	★ ★ ★ ★ ★
AU		

There is an awful lot of content to this site and the long homepage is quite crowded with Important Notices, a review of the site, links to other writing links, a list of other contents on the site, and a few advertising banners. With so many sites to choose from, it doesn't really grab you immediately and encourage you to go much further. Which would be a terrible shame, as there is a wealth of simply excellent content. So, by all means, browse the first page, but finally settle on either of the white navigation boxes, one at the top, one at the bottom. This way you won't miss anything.

SPECIAL FEATURES

Articles Some excellent articles about a variety of writing topics. The titles alone are pretty good and make you want to read on. Titles include 'Starting a Freelance Writing Career Online', How to Find a Publisher' and 'Contest Junkie'. If you're ready to soak up even more writing help and knowledge, click on the Archives link on this page and you can access every single article that has appeared in the Writers Exchange Ezine. More of the Ezine below.

Writing Links So many links so little time. The danger with this number of links is that you can spend an entire writing day just browsing and not write a single word of your own. What is good here is that before you get to the links themselves, they have been very sensibly sorted into categories. So, if you want Writing Contests or Writing Jobs and Markets, you can click the appropriate section and only see relevant links on the following page which will save you loads of time.

Jobs/Markets The largest page of links to sites offering actual openings to writers that we've seen. If you're serious about getting a position as a writer then this is exactly what you want. Most of the sites are based in America, but many carry jobs from around the world. Some jobs you may be able to do from home, via the internet.

Ezine Archives Fantastic web-based monthly magazine, which is no longer being produced. However, the columnists are still writing for the site and the back issues are full to bursting with excellent articles, reviews and columns. The first year's articles have recently been published as an ebook which you can buy online.

OTHER FEATURES

Ask The Experts Five experts, specialising in specific genres will answer your writing questions.

Author Interviews A handful of professional writers let you under their skin.

Authors Homepages Fancy a whole page of your own to advertise your books? Lots of writers already have them. Email the site for further details. This won't even cost you any money, just a link back to the site, if you have your own web site. Sounds like a great deal.

Writing Books E-Publishing Buy ebooks, published by Writers Exchange. There are also book and software reviews and advice columns.

Great advice from writers for writers. A great, but sadly missed, Ezine. Time spent here is well spent.

www.writing-world.com
Writing World

Overall rating: ★ ★ ★ ★ ★			
Classification:	Guide	**Content:**	★ ★ ★ ★ ★
Updating:	Regularly	**Readability:**	★ ★ ★ ★ ★
Navigation:	★ ★ ★ ★	**Speed:**	★ ★ ★ ★ ★

(US)

Big site. Covers everything concerned with writing. To give you some idea of the range of tips and articles, recent articles posted were 'Checking the Quality of your Translated Book' and 'Creating a Realistic Fantasy World'. It has one of those homepages that scrolls on and on down the page, occasionally making you feel you'll have to stumble across the best bits of the site rather than being shown, clearly, where they are. They wait until you're at the very bottom before providing all the section links in one place. However, this is not a site about navigation but about writing, which is something they excel in. The homepage is basically three columns, the two blue ones are basically links to places of interest outside of Writing World. The middle column is the one you want. Half way down, the different section links begin, with a few sub-headings so you know what to expect. Expect great advice, in easily accessible terms, and prepare for your writing, at the very least, to improve.

SPECIAL FEATURES

Getting Started Many sites have only a couple of articles for the complete beginner. Very often they simply discuss writing in very basic terms. But not here. At the time of writing there were almost 50 articles, and further links for beginners at the bottom of the page. You are in very safe hands here. Learn the basics in a professional way, without being mollycoddled.

Rights, Contracts and Copyright Many people simply write for their own pleasure. If you want to make money from your writing and make a career of it, there are lots of legal considerations you will need to apply to your work and your writing life. This section is an area often overlooked on writing sites, but is terribly important. Articles cover electronic rights, International rights, and what to do if you don't get paid for a piece of work. Excellent.

Fiction The beauty of this section is that it contains specific articles for writing genres, including Romance, Science Fiction and Fantasy, and Horror. There are further links to other sites covering these genres too.

International Resources Another section with articles you don't often see. Keep in mind that this is not a UK site, hence the articles on writing for UK markets. Translation is covered, as is the exciting prospect of Running an International Writing Business.

Promoting Your Writing You've written it, but how do you get anyone to read it? There's a regular column on the subject and almost a dozen other articles to help you along.

Advanced Writing Tips Is there no end to the superb features on this site? It seems not. Here, you can find out how to make that first contact with a writing market really work for you. Also includes business advice, selling reprints, and lots of additional resources.

Other Features There are other useful sections and columns on General Writing, Publishing, Freelancing, Children's Writing, Poetry, the Business side of writing, Classes, Markets, Contests and Greeting cards. All contain articles and more links. If you have any time left after all that lot, sign up for the free newsletter. Authors can also promote there books on the site for a small fee.

Superb site. Excellent content. If you can't find the help you want here, it may not be available anywhere on planet earth.

www.momwriters.com
Momwriters

Overall rating: ★★★★		
Classification: Community	**Content:**	★★★★
Updating: Monthly	**Readability:**	★★★★
Navigation: ★★★	**Speed:**	★★★★★

(US)

Traditionally the writer is seen as a solitary figure, locked away in a small room, writing or typing out a masterpiece with no distractions other than the murmuring of their muse. The reality is more likely to involve trying to fit in writing around a full time job, a relationship, a domestic life and possibly lots of shrieking children running around, with questions, disruptions and a frightening number of sticky fingers. Writing and children are difficult to mix, but this site is dedicated to those brave enough to try.

Click Come On In for the Homepage. It's a very long Homepage, but the neat purple buttons around the funky header take you quickly where you want to go. However, browsing is encouraged as there is so much to see. The site has had an overhaul recently and all the changes are for the better.

SPECIAL FEATURES

Projects There's loads on offer: pen friends for your kids; gifts to buy; clubs; a critique group; guidelines and even a fund to help out Momwriters in need. Classes are coming soon too.

Resources An excellent array of links presented in an easy to follow way, with brief descriptions of what to expect when you get there. A wealth of sites offer information on Markets, Beginners Info, Guidelines and much, much more. Very useful.

All About Momwriters Find out who's behind all this and how to contact them. There are a few house rules you should check out, a chat room, bulletin board, and a link where you can join the very busy Momwriters Listserve.

Resources Whether a new writer or an old hand, you'll find lots of useful information here. Chats with authors; the nuts and bolts of a writing career; help with Character Development, and Fees, as well as a host of guidelines and Markets to help you sell what you write.

Momwriters Write Tips, questions answered, details of books published by members of the site. There are lots of columns and so much help, you'll have no excuses for not getting down to some writing of your own. But what? Check out the Writing Exercises link at the bottom of the page for loads of thought provoking stuff to get you going and kick start your creativity.

Other Features Contests, Awards, Spotlight on Fellow Momwriters and lots and lots more.

A great community that gives recognition, help and encouragement to all writer/parents.

www.oneofus.co.uk/index.htm			
One of Us			
Overall rating: ★★★★			
Classification:	Guide	Content:	★★★★
Updating:	Occasionally	Readability:	★★★★★
Navigation:	★★★★★	Speed:	★★★★★
UK			

www.wakeupwriting.com/index.html			
Wake Up Writing			
Overall rating: ★★★★			
Classification:	Homepage	Content:	★★★★
Updating:	Daily	Readability:	★★★★★
Navigation:	★★★★★	Speed:	★★★★★
US			

This site has at its heart, what most good writing has – simplicity. The site is about information, so there's no fussing about with graphics or download-heavy design. Yet it still looks great. It's based in the UK, so, for a change, it's a site which is pleasantly biased towards the British writer. You'll find the links on the left of every page you visit. On the homepage use the tabs at the top to reach the different sections. It's all held together by one writer, but you are encouraged to get involved, send in your tips, and basically join in.

SPECIAL FEATURES

writing tips Straightforward advice and tips, articles and writing exercises, many of them sent in by visitors to the site.

Writers' Directory Lots of writing groups, links to sites, books, software, and even writers' personal sites, where you can read their work, network, or just browse.

Other Features A variety of articles covering everything from plot to the responsibilities of being a writer. There's also a selection of stories sent in by visitors to the site (however submissions are no longer being accepted.

British, simple, concise, useful.

One of the most important bits of advice you can ever be given as a writer is to keep writing. No matter how much you don't feel like it. No matter how badly your latest project is going. No matter how strongly writer's block has taken hold. Write, write anything, but write. This site makes sure you do just that. Every weekday you can sit at your computer, with your first mug of coffee of the day, and read the writing exercise that's been set for you. This will get your mind thinking creatively and, most importantly, it will make sure you begin to get words down on paper. There is no right way to complete the exercises and no one will mark them or even look at them for you. They are simply a method to get your creativity flowing. No matter what genre you are interested in, these exercises really will help.

It's a very sunny, brightly designed site, with just enough colour to help you feel lively without giving you a headache. Running up the centre of the screen are the exercises for the last five days. Simply click the link to be taken to the exercise in full. Other site links can be found in the orange column on the left, with additional resources at the very bottom of the homepage.

SPECIAL FEATURES

Exercises If today's exercise doesn't inspire you, click here for weeks and weeks worth of previous exercises, at the time of writing there were more than 150 to be going on with.

Just follow the simple instructions and watch the words flow from your pen or keyboard.

Links Small selection of sites to help your writing productivity and creativity.

Free Update Subscribe, so you don't miss out on any of the good stuff that happens here. Absolutely free.

Other Features Links, news about a few ezines and a feedback page.

A great 'push' to get you writing.

---

www.writersmanual.com
Writers Manual

Overall rating: ★ ★ ★ ★			
Classification:	Guide	**Content:**	★ ★ ★ ★
Updating:	Weekly	**Readability:**	★ ★ ★ ★ ★
Navigation:	★ ★ ★ ★ ★	**Speed:**	★ ★ ★ ★ ★

US

Just glancing through this Good Web Guide will underline that there are is no shortage of sites offering all manner of excellent writing advice. This is yet another one. It's American, as so many of the good writing sites seem to be. What makes this one slightly different from many of the others, is the variety of writers who will find interesting information. On the day of writing, the homepage alone had advice for writers who: also have other full time jobs; article writers; journalists; thriller novelists; self publishers; home writers; song lyricists, as well as a mass of resources for these and every other type of writer imaginable. The look of the site is like that of a busy noticeboard, there are site links at the top of the left column, the rest of the homepage is peppered with ads from site sponsors and links to other helpful sites. None of this detracts, however, from the fact that there is plenty here for all writers. Everything is offered to you for free, but if you do get a lot from it, they are more than happy for you to place their banner on your site and give them a little more exposure.

SPECIAL FEATURES

Articles There is always more you can learn about the craft of writing and of promoting yourself as a professional. Therefore you should never tire of soaking up more information from intelligently written pieces like these. However, we would recommend that you don't read all the articles in one sitting, as there are masses and they have actually been turned into a site of their own. Follow the link. This is where most UK writers will want to keep coming back to.

Book Picks Need more info? Try these recommended titles. As always, search for these on a UK site rather than trying to order them all the way from the USA. It's just easier and makes more sense.

Book Reviews The pick of the books are reviewed. You won't find so much as a single word said against any of them.

Other Features Sign up for free email updates containing information and announcements. There's also a short list of contests, a huge list of links to jobs online, and an outrageous amount of links to other sites, that might take you the rest of your working life to wade through. Also ebooks looking for submissions, from you.

Lots of articles offering help and inspiration to all kinds of writers.

www.writerswrite.com
Writers Write

Overall rating: ★★★★		
Classification: Resource	**Content:**	★★★★
Updating: Daily	**Readability:**	★★★★★
Navigation: ★★★★	**Speed:**	★★★★★

US

Huge site that sets itself apart from many other writing sites by the sheer variety of writing and writers it covers. It's in existence to help you improve your writing, whatever level you're at. There are jobs, book reviews, interviews, 21 fairly active message boards, a great speciality section, excellent resources and a huge writers marketplace. The long homepage has tasters of what's in store and, on the left, the blue navigation bar to take you to the various sections.

SPECIAL FEATURES

The IWJ Subscribe for free to this excellent monthly journal. You'll find author interviews, and features and articles on all manner of writing topics from a variety of experts who know what they're talking about.

Speciality Sections This section is really a portal to other sites featuring advice and information. The sections include Business Writing, Greeting Cards, Screenwriting, Poetry, Journalism and even Song Writing. Lots of links, with really useful little blurbs so you know what to expect and aren't wasting your time.

Resources A huge library of links to everything you might need as a writer. From news, book publishing, computers and articles, to webrings, conferences, writing groups and writing organisations.

The Write News All the latest for writing industry professionals and those who want to remain in the know.

Readers Read Meet with other readers online and discuss your favourite books.

Author Interviews More than a hundred conversations with writing professionals, every one of them talking about things that are interesting and useful for writers to hear.

Jobs and Markets for Writers Under this umbrella heading are links to job listings, paying markets and a list of writers looking for work.

Writer's Marketplace A fairly long list of ads. Writers and companies selling their services, newsletters, seminars. A short explanation and contact details are supplied.

Community Chat, loads of fairly busy, genre related, message boards, and a forum to air all your opinions on the pressing writing issues of the day.

Research Links to help you deal with online research. Help with search engines, surfing and more.

A large, detailed site. Great variety and content.

---

http://groups.yahoo.com/
Yahoo! Groups

Overall rating: ★★★★		
Classification: Community	**Content:**	★★★★
Updating: Frequently	**Readability:**	★★★★★
Navigation: ★★★★	**Speed:**	★★★★★

US

So much of the internet, and especially the writing part of the internet, is made up of communities. Like minded people get together, debate, chat, argue, swap ideas and discuss whatever it is that they have in common. For writers that can mean other writers creating in the same genre; people who like the same writers, books and films or any number of other topics.

But there is also another use for these communities for writers. Research. Where better to look for information on a particular topic than in a community populated by potential experts, and at the very least, keen amateurs in the field? Exactly.

This site has massive lists of such groups. Some of the groups are actually ezines or newsletters, other are forums for discussion where members post their opinions and comment on other member's views.

Maybe you should sit down before we tell you that there are currently 16 sections of groups ranging from Business and Finance to Romance and Relationships. From a writing point of view you want the Entertainment and Arts section. Still sitting down? This section alone contains more than 135,000 groups.

Within this section, writers want to click on the Humanities link, and then on the Books and Writing link on the next page. Yea, that's the one. The one that contains more than

12000 groups. You will see that the Writing link alone houses more than 3000 groups.

Some of the groups have thousands of members, others have just a handful. They are ordered by the number of members each group has, so the most popular ones will always be at the top.

If you're after something very specific, try using the search facility to see relevant groups.

If you find something that appeals to you, you can apply to join by following the online instructions. Many of the lists have websites too which is especially useful when researching, as it's even easier to find an email address to send your research requests to.

And finally, if the list you were after doesn't exist, why not start it yourself by clicking the Start a New Group link?

A phenomenal number of groups with an unbelievable number of participants.

OTHER SITES OF INTEREST

The Art Of Writing
http://www.artofwritingzine.com/

A quarterly magazine available on the web. It's a little messy, in that navigation is not at all clear. To find many of the links, go to the Free Clipart section and some will miraculously appear. The site has recently undergone some changes and there are still wrinkles to be ironed out. However, it does have Five Golden Rules for Writers, which is excellent. You'll also find a wonderful Instant Inspiration device which randomly generates the basics of a short story or the first line of a poem. You can email the piece to the magazine when it's finished. Great for kick starting your muse.

Robin's Nest
http://robinsnest.com/index.html

Not a 1970s situation comedy, but an attractive site run by a freelance writer. The Writers section is the link to click. Here you will find lots of really good links to subjects including Crime, Publishers and Agents, Children's writing, Grammar, Journalists, Romance and more. There are also a number of online workshops and course, which are there in their entirety and offer detailed help and advice on lots of topics.

The Society of Authors
www.society of authors.org

Established in 1884 and with 7000 members, this society helps to protect the interests of writers by offering detailed advice on all the business side of being a writer. Some of these include copyright, accountancy, tax and libel. Members are also entitled to receive a series of Quick Guides covering lots of subjects relevant to a writer, including Indexing, Agents and Film Agreements. There is also a searchable database of all the members. Membership is open to professional writers. Check the Membership page for a full list of details. A first years membership is available for £75 and payment is made by post.

Writer's Cramp
www.writerscramp.ca

There's something about reading quality writing that inspires you, makes you want to improve your own. This site is simple and yet very attractively designed. It is filled with intelligent prose, poetry, essays and opinion. There's a sharp, lively humour that runs through the site, which doesn't allow you to feel out of your depth amidst all this talent. You can also expect to find some interesting writing links and archives of previous editions. But most of all, you'll enjoy well written pieces, the quality of which will have you striving to match it and submit something of your own.

Writers Resource Centre
http://www.poewar.com/index.html

Very simply designed site that basically has a collection of articles running up the home page. They have the sort of encouraging titles that convince you they'll make a difference to your writing. Titles like, Creating Memorable Characters; 10 Tips For Writing Your Mystery Novel; and Compiling Quizzes. The articles are nicely specific and cover not only the Craft of writing, but also Technology and Business. You'll also find book reviews and links to ten other useful writing sites.

Chapter 03
getting published

Even if you begin writing for nothing more than the pleasure you get from it, at some time you will almost certainly toy with idea of being published. Whether it's a letter to an Editor, a short story, an article, a novel or an Oscar winning, multimillion pound Hollywood Blockbuster that smashes all known records; however big your ambition, you'll do well to get a little advice before you begin.

Many of the sites in this chapter point you in the direction of markets. Many of those markets are in America. For some unknown reason, these foreign markets put UK writers off. It shouldn't. With the benefit of email, a magazine, publisher or production company are only as far away as your computer. The whole world is a market place. Use it.

Other sites will help you self-publish, or advertise your work on their sites. Some are basically looking for new talent. If you want your writing to be anything more than just a hobby, these sites will introduce you to the big, bad world of getting published and making money.

www.authorlink.com			
Authorlink			
Overall rating: ★★★★			
Classification:	Marketplace	Content:	★★★★★
Updating:	Frequently	Readability:	★★★
Navigation:	★★★	Speed:	★★★★★
US			

If you're having trouble coming up with ideas, creativity all dried up, or if you want guidance on how to write that masterpiece, you've come to the wrong place. However, if the masterpiece is finished and you want to give it the maximum exposure to agents and publishers, grab a coffee, sit yourself down and get stuck into this excellent site. More than 250,000 readers visit this online clearing house site each year, and those, oh so busy agents and publishers check out more than two million pages in the same time. Authorlink also has its own publishing company, which they are quick to assure you has nothing to do with vanity publishing. What they do, is evaluate your work, and if it is of a high enough standard they will list on their site your resume, synopsis and an excerpt. They'll charge you for the service, but at $56 for three months inclusion, it is pretty good value. Even if this doesn't appeal to you there is lots available for free, including industry news, resources columns and articles.

The site is not simple to get around. Sometimes it is positively clumsy. Just about every word on the homepage can be clicked. There are links in the blue and brown band across the top of the page. Bold rectangles down the left indicate further links. The blue industry news headlines can be clicked for the full story. More links at the bottom. Many of these links are repeated from place to place. It's the one horrible thing in an otherwise great site.

SPECIAL FEATURES

Submission Guidelines & FAQs Available from the blue band at the top of the page. Whatever you do, read this section first. It's very detailed and will leave you in no doubt about whether their paying services are for you. It tells you who they are, what they do, how much it costs, what you can send and how to send it. Exceptionally excellent section, leaves nothing to your imagination.

Create New Account If you decide you want to be considered for a listing, you'll need this link. As usual, you are guided through the process and the clarity couldn't be better.

Articles/Columns/Reviews Information, advice and interview. Page design again detracts from good content. To get to all the articles, click the Articles! Articles! Articles! Link, top right in this section.

Writer's Resources Includes publishing guidelines, a writer's store, links to other sites and organisations and a mish-mash of links to give you a mild headache.

Other Features Thankfully there's a search facility if you can't find something in particular. A smallish jobs section has predominantly American jobs on offer. You can put your own small ad in for free, for 30 days. The jobs section also includes a very detailed list of possible markets. You can also buy books from the site and read more about Authorlink by clicking the Authorlink News/Info link, half way down the homepage, on the left.

Great service, great features, if you can find it all before losing patience.

www.becomingawriter.co.uk
Becoming A Writer

Overall rating: ★★★★★			
Classification:	Guide	**Content:**	★★★★★
Updating:	Monthly	**Readability:**	★★★★★
Navigation:	★★★★★	**Speed:**	★★★★★

UK

This site is like having a wiser and more experienced friend sitting by your side when you're writing, thinking about writing or simply daydreaming about being a successful writer. It's a very nicely designed site, very fresh and modern and purple. It is aimed at story writers, rather than poets, script writers or journalists. However, if you want to be a writer, want to get published, or simply don't want to feel you're all on your own as a writer, help is well and truly at hand.

SPECIAL FEATURES

Newsletter The mainstay of the site. Simply fill in your name and email address and the newsletter will be emailed to you for free once a month. You will find a wonderful grounding in all the basics of finding ideas, understanding the business, constructing the basic elements of a good story and more. There's never too much to take in at one time, so you will never feel overwhelmed. It's so laid back and easy to read that it's simply a wonderful first step to becoming a writer.

Writer's Path Here you are taken gently by the hand and given an explanation of what you're up against on the road to being a writer. It describes the main qualities you'll need and the steps you'll have to take. There are a number of tips to help you along the way.

OTHER FEATURES

Book Reviews A small selection of helpful titles that you can buy online from Amazon.co.uk .

Friendly and informative. Especially good for those just starting out as writers.

www.booklocker.com
Booklocker

Overall rating: ★ ★ ★ ★ ★			
Classification:	E-Publisher	Content:	★ ★ ★ ★
Updating:	Daily	Readability:	★ ★ ★ ★ ★
Navigation:	★ ★ ★ ★ ★	Speed:	★ ★ ★ ★ ★

US

Is this the future of publishing? Time will tell. Booklocker sell ebooks and Print on Demand (POD) books for self-publishing authors. Briefly, an ebook, is your manuscript in electronic form, that is downloaded, for a fee, from the internet and viewed using an Adobe Acrobat Reader, which is free to download from the net. A POD book is one that is only printed as the demand requires. There will be no copies of your book lying around in a warehouse, if an order comes in for ten copies, or even a single copy, then that's how many they print, until the next order comes in. No waste, which means less expense to you, the writer. Obviously, these POD books are in print, rather than electronic form and, unfortunately, are only available for delivery in the USA.

On the front page, the first thing you are greeted with is a list of the top ten selling books at the site. Click around to see the types of books that are selling. If you want to browse further, use the Select a Category drop-down box at the top of the page and browse the print books available by category. It's a simply designed site, that shows off the books weil and provides a decent service for authors and readers alike.

SPECIAL FEATURES

Authors Click Here This is where you will find everything you need to know about getting your book on the site. Everything is explained concisely and clearly. Make sure you follow Read More links to get further information, and then the Ready For The Fine Print links so you have the entire picture. Bear in mind that they don't simply take every book that's sent to them, so if yours is accepted it should be in some pretty high quality company. And, just in case you were wondering, yes authors will make money from the sale of both print and ebooks. Don't worry about this being an American site. They already have many non-US authors and treat everyone as 'part of the family'.

Book Ordering/Delivery If you want to know the exact process of downloading a book, read this, then all will be revealed.

OTHER FEATURES

As it will only take a few moments, remember to read the FAQ, which will help answer any further questions you might have.

If you want to self publish, this is an excellent site to consider.

www.egroodies.com/Athens/Rhodes/3575/wn/wlastex4home.html			
The New Writer's Network			
Overall rating: ★ ★ ★ ★ ★			
Classification:	Guide	**Content:**	★ ★ ★ ★ ★
Updating:	Frequently	**Readability:**	★ ★ ★ ★ ★
Navigation:	★ ★ ★ ★ ★	**Speed:**	★ ★ ★ ★ ★
US			

The moment you begin reading the homepage, you will be in no doubt about what to expect here: 'the complete guide for aspiring authors to see their work in print.' What this consists of is a wonderfully useful list of contacts who are willing to look at new writing. This includes publishers, magazines and agents. Most of them are in the UK. You get names, address, phone and fax numbers and email addresses. Everything you need to get your writing out there, in front of the people who matter.

If you need a bit of help before you send your pages out, there are articles to guide you. One of the most useful parts of the site includes a form you can fill in yourself, to report changes to the entries and to comment on your experience as a new writer approaching these contacts. Extremely useful.

Click the red buttons on the left of the homepage to get around easily.

SPECIAL FEATURES

FAQ Always a good place to start. Answers, as all FAQ sections should, the most obvious questions you'll ask while browsing.

Publishers Currently the list contains more than 60 publishers. There are even details of whether the company was willing to view a manuscript written and submitted to them by the site owner.

Agents Just short of 90 agents. You'll find all the contact details you need and a slowly growing list of comments from other writers who have approached them.

Magazines Small selection of magazines organised by genre, including New Age, Art, Travel and Fiction.

Submission Follow the advice here, before submitting a manuscript and you will greatly increase your chances of a getting over the first hurdle. Includes advice about paper, formatting, alterations and an extremely useful list of things to consider when submitting a non-fiction manuscript.

Feedback The all important where you and fellow writers help to keep the site up to date and growing. The form is very simple to use and prompts you for the information they want. Couldn't be simpler.

OTHER FEATURES

An interesting section on Design, especially with regard to web pages, to improve your site and impress more people with it. There's also a fairly large section of links for writers, if you have any to add, they're more than happy to receive them. There are also growing lists of US Publishers and US Agents, to whom you can submit to.

User friendly and user useful. Is sure to grow into an essential, up to date resource.

www.little-magazines.org.uk
Little Magazines

Overall rating: ★ ★ ★ ★		
Classification: Resource	**Content:**	★ ★ ★ ★ ★
Updating: Monthly	**Readability:**	★ ★ ★ ★ ★
Navigation: ★ ★ ★	**Speed:**	★ ★ ★ ★ ★

(UK)

When you are first starting out, and indeed for most writers at any stage of their careers, there can be enormous frustration when approaching the bigger magazines and publications, trying to place your work. This is especially true when trying to sell a story. Therefore it is worth remembering that there are dozens of other, smaller magazines, who do not receive quite the avalanche of submissions and therefore can perhaps provide a better opportunity for writers looking for their first published credit. Of course, this does not mean that your submissions can be any less professional, any less thought out or sub-standard in any way. It may mean, however, that if you have a piece of work accepted there may be little or nothing in the way of payment. However, if one of these magazines allows you to see your work in print for the first time, will money really be an issue? You can always put off worrying about making a living from writing for some other time.

This site has collected together the details of more than 100 of these smaller magazines, all based in the UK. Each entry has contact details and web links where appropriate. It is an extremely simple, clear site and yet slightly frustrating as you have to click each magazine title to see what genres they publish. And it's a long list. A little categorisation would be a great help. Some links lead directly to the publisher's website, others simple give you the relevant magazine details.

SPECIAL FEATURES

What's New This is where to click first to see the latest inclusions, the titles that have closed down and any changes in entry details.

Links If you can't find specific information in the site contents, you will almost certainly get lucky by following some of these excellent links. The links lead to Communities, Ezines, Small Presses and Resources and contain dozens of mostly British sites with masses of information for writers.

Other Features A Shop recommends a small number of titles, all linked to Amazon.co.uk.

The site content and the excellent links make this a wonderful site for the less mainstream market, although design may mean a lot of browsing before you get what you want.

www.writersdigest.com		
Writer's Digest		
Overall rating: ★★★★★		
Classification: Magazine	Content:	★★★★
Updating: Daily	Readability:	★★★★★
Navigation: ★★★★★	Speed:	★★★★★
(US)		

If you have ever searched the 'creative writing' shelves of your local bookshop, you will almost certainly have come across the Writer's Digest as a book publisher. Likewise, their magazine is available in most decent sized newsagents. And now, if you check out writing sites on the internet, it won't be long before someone recommends them as a link you should click. It might be because they've been around since 1921, which would suggest they've ironed out any teething troubles and know what they've doing. This site is dedicated to those writing for books and magazines.

They're very American. Which shouldn't be a problem, but we know it occasionally puts people off when a site is almost exclusively 'non-UK', thinking that they are possibly wasting their time at a site which has nothing for them. However, a little something to remember is that good writing advice is relevant, no matter what accent it's given in. Also, although most of the markets are American, who's to say they won't buy your work? The internet is shrinking the world, take advantage of all the International markets, before everyone else does.

The site is simple in design and the colours are generally pastel which makes a big difference to your eyes after you've been browsing for a long time.

To get around, simply click on the links on the left of the page. For you convenience these links are available from each subsequent page too.

SPECIAL FEATURES

Hot List A list of the top 100 markets for selling your writing with email and web site addresses where appropriate. Not surprisingly, most of them are in the USA.

Writer's Guidelines Absolutely superb list of hundreds of writer's guidelines. Many of these entries give you exactly what the particular publication would send you if you had contacted them directly. Use the search drop down box at the bottom of the page to choose your area of interest, and the keyword box if you want to be very specific. Again, expect very little non-American content.

From this page you can also sign up for the excellent Writer's Market newsletter which includes submission tips from editors, market information, formatting guidelines for your work as well as insider information about the publishing industry and updates on new products for writers.

OTHER FEATURES

Contests A smallish collection of competitions for all types of creative writing.

Books Lots and lots of books to help your writing. However, if you find something you want, we recommend you search for it at a British book store like, www.amazon.co.uk .

If you want to break into the American Magazine market, this is a superb resource.

www.writersmarket.com/index_ns.asp
Writer's Market.com

Overall rating: ★★★★★		
Classification: Guide	**Content:**	★★★★★
Updating: Frequently	**Readability:**	★★★★★
Navigation: ★★★★	**Speed:**	★★★★★

(US)

As we all know, much of the information on the internet is available for nothing. It's rare to find a site that charges you for membership, but actually lives up to the fee. But this is one such site. It is the online version of the American publication Writer's Market which has been 'the writer's bible' since 1921. Basically it has collected together more than 4000 places where writers can market their work, including book publishers, magazines, contests, greeting card companies, scriptwriting markets, as well as a large database of literary agents. You'll find, names, addresses, phone numbers and other contact details. They also keep their details up to date, which is a huge improvement on many contacts sites. Useful for writing professionals and those just beginning.

Add to this, a new column by a professional literary agent, a Submission Tracker (see below), a great search facility, free newsletters and the ability to customise parts of the site to your own interests, make this an all round winner. The design is simple but efficient, navigation easy and everything loads pretty quickly too.

However, like we said, it's not free. A year's subscription will cost $29.99 a year or $2.99 a month, payable by credit card via a secure server, so you needn't worry about giving out your card details. In the UK you would be charged in US dollars, then debited in sterling according to the exchange rate. Available now is the 2002 Writer's Market Online edition, which is a companion book that also includes online access to the website included in the price. Inside the book you'll find an activation code and directions of how to get to the online registration form where the code is used to initiate your subscription. Current subscribers can renew their subscription in the same way. This book is currently available from Amazon.co.uk for a very reasonable £31, which works out less than eight and a half pence a day, which you should easily make back after a single sale.

SPECIAL FEATURES

Your Writer's Market This is where the writing markets that particularly interest you can be managed. Create your own Favourite Folders so you can quickly keep track of any market changes. Excellent, up to the minute information.

Submission Tracker A wonderful tool for managing your writing submissions. It is so easy to lose track of what was sent where and when, but this feature makes sure you'll never forget again. Particularly useful for writers of articles or short pieces, but can be used to stay on top of any form of writing submissions. And if you're quite happy keeping details of your submissions with a pen and pad, just consider for a moment whether, after a couple of moments your pen and pad can find you new markets with all the relevant contact details at the click of a button. Thought not.

Encyclopedia 1300 entries means virtually anything you could want to know about the world of writing is covered here from AA (author's alteration) to Zeitgeist. More useful than you can imagine.

OTHER FEATURES

Search Markets A powerful, yet simple search engine to find you market information quickly.

Tips Library Find articles and advice on a whole range of writing categories. No frantic searching, simply choose the area you want help on from a drop down box. Simple and very useful.

If you want to sell to America, this guide is simply invaluable.

www.adlerbooks.com			
Adler & Robin Books			
Overall rating: ★★★★			
Classification:	Agency/Publisher	Content:	★★★★★
Updating:	Fortnightly	Readability:	★★★
Navigation:	★★★★	Speed:	★★★★★
US			

Adler & Robin Books is a lot of things. It's a literary agency, a book packager and also a publisher in its own right. Bill Adler, he of the company name, is also a bestselling author of such wondrously titled books as 'Outwitting Squirrels', 'Baby-English: A Dictionary for Interpreting the Secret Language of Infants' and 'Outwitting Fish'. However, what makes this site stand out is its always enthusiastic tone and its willingness to offer writers help instead of merely coming across as a 'profit and nothing else' kind of company.

The site design is not the most original. Apart from the occasional page changeover which glides, or spirals from one page to the next, (click around to find them) it's rather plain, but pages load quickly and navigation, although not pretty, is simple. For all the site's navigational links, simply scroll down the homepage and the blue type tells you what to expect. New pages have further interesting links at the bottom, but to get the full and complete links list you'll have to use the Back button on your browser.

SPECIAL FEATURES

Submission Guidelines Possibly the most important part of the site. They don't hold it against you if you are not an American, but make sure you digest these guidelines fully before submitting anything to one of their agents. They have over 5000 queries a year. Good luck.

How to Write a ... Book Proposal Two links, one for Computer and one for Trade proposals. Lots to consider but presented in a brief, easy to follow, almost step by step format.

The best of the worst book ideas Visitors to the site are invited to send in titles of dreadful non-fiction books that will never see the publishing light of day. Can you compete with 'Hot Dogs: Why Aren't They Green Instead?'

How to Promote Your Book Invaluable information on how you can go about getting more people to buy more copies of your books.

Most Asked Questions of Literary Agents Excellent FAQ page detailing everything you ever wanted to know about those guys who take a percentage of everything you earn.

OTHER FEATURES

There are a number of invitations to help the company with research for forthcoming books. At the time of writing these included books about your first kiss, hospital safety and a book about Outwitting Clutter. You'll also find links to the American Amazon site where copies of their published titles can be found. As always, if you're not in the US, search for the titles at Amazon.co.uk, or another UK online bookseller. There are also a variety of extremely useful, stand-alone articles including ways to back up your computer data, warnings about Print on Demand books and Book Writing Guidelines. Also very useful are the four sample book proposals. See how yours should look before sending it off.

Enthusiastic, friendly site that might even go so far as to publish your book.

---

www.inscriptionsmagazine.com/Home.html
Inscriptions

Overall rating: ★★★★			
Classification:	Ezine	Content:	★★★★
Updating:	Weekly	Readability:	★★★★
Navigation:	★★★★	Speed:	★★★★★

US

'The weekly ezine for professional writers'. Each issue features articles on different types of writing, job opportunities, markets you can try and sell your work to, contests, book reviews and more. Again, this site is predominantly filled with American content, but as is mentioned elsewhere in these pages, the whole world is a market, not just your home country, and good advice is good advice, no matter what the nationality of the advice giver. The site has recently switched to a paying subscription, but at only $5 (US) it's little more than a donation to aid the running costs of the sites. This is money well spent when you see the extent of your weekly ezine. Click Subscribe at the bottom of the homepage to sign up and for ways to pay. The ezine arrives as a text only document, but if you want to read the current content in a slightly more stylish design, click the links at each of the four corners of the Inscriptions homepage logo.

SPECIAL FEATURES

Search Inscriptions It's the main feature of the homepage and responds very quickly to your search criteria. However, the results are simply presented with a link and the opening to the article to give you a taste of what's in store.

Archives Read past issues of this excellent ezine.

OTHER FEATURES

Professional Opportunities Jobs, Markets and Contests.

Hone your craft Articles, news, obituaries, tip of the week and dead markets.

Digital Muse Get your creative juices flowing again with a variety of links.

Wide variety of writing topics for professional and aspiring writers.

www.thepublishedwriter.com			
The Published Writer			
Overall rating: ★ ★ ★			
Classification:	Ezine	Content:	★ ★ ★ ★ ★
Updating:	Weekly	Readability:	★ ★ ★ ★ ★
Navigation:	★ ★ ★ ★ ★	Speed:	★ ★ ★ ★ ★
(PH)			

This site is aimed at giving unpublished writers all the information and help they need to get into print. There are interviews with authors, success stories, as well as news headlines from the world of writing. The design is fairly simple, without the colourful backgrounds that make some sites hard work on the eyes. It loads quickly and navigation is via the green column on the left. It's a fairly new site that only began in March 2001, but it's growing all the time with a whole series of 'You can be...' writing articles, and there are more author interviews promised soon.

SPECIAL FEATURES

Articles A shortish collection of articles about a variety of writing issues. Recent subjects have included the pitfalls of paying an agent, coping with rejection and a ten part article on becoming a greeting card writer.

Writing News Links to writing stories from around the world.

Links Long list of writing related sites with a very useful description of what to expect if you go there.

Free Update Make sure you're kept up to date with all the changes at the site with this free ezine. Just let them have your name and email address.

Links Speaks for itself and provides links to the homepages of a variety of sites who specialise variously in Children's,

Christian, Fantasy, Poetry and Romance publishing and more. There are sites that deal with plagiarism, technical writing, epublishing and a host of other interesting subjects.

It's early days for this site, but it is already friendly, informative and growing.

www.writers.net
Writer's Net

Overall rating: ★★★★			
Classification:	Directory	**Content:**	★★★★
Updating:	Constantly	**Readability:**	★★★★★
Navigation:	★★★★★	**Speed:**	★★★★

US

If you are a writer, agent, publisher or an editor, then this site will be of great interest to you. You can happily add yourself and your writing credits to the database, where other members of the site can browse and find you, and if you're a published writer, maybe buy your book. If you are looking for someone in one of these categories to represent you, publish you or help you with a project, the database is easy to search. Register to make full use of the site. It's free and you can even get your own Writer's Net email address, if you want.

The homepage has lots of topical links to the writing articles and thoughts of the day. Further down is a brief description of what they're about. However, to navigate with ease, choose the blue buttons at the top of the homepage.

SPECIAL FEATURES

Writers Find a writer or add to your online portfolio. There's a lot to be said for seeing your name and details on the internet and knowing millions of others can see them too. Who knows, it may result in the break you're looking for, it might do, but don't hold your breath.

Agents Literary agents can help you sell your work and shape your career. Currently, you can search geographically to find, amongst others, 35 agents in the UK and 403 in the USA. This isn't anywhere near as complete a list as you might find in The Writer's Handbook, but at least all these agents have actively chosen to be on the site and might look upon you favourably.

Editors and Publishers You can add your entry, or search through the lists, again by type or location.

OTHER FEATURES

Resources A fairly substantial list of recommended books for writers. Clicking their title takes you to Amazon in America, so if you want a book and don't live in The States, look for it at Amazon.co.uk instead.

Discussion Fairly lively forums that have individual message boards for each of the four categories represented on the site, as well as one for Unpublished Writers and one for the discussion of the Writing Craft. Very chatty community. Make sure to read the Terms and Conditions of Use first.

Nice site, very easy to use with a friendly community feel.

www.writersguild.org.uk
Writer's Guild of Great Britain

Overall rating: ★ ★ ★ ★

Classification:	Trade Union	Content:	★ ★ ★ ★
Updating:	Occasionally	Readability:	★ ★ ★ ★
Navigation:	★ ★ ★ ★ ★	Speed:	★ ★ ★ ★ ★

UK

'Membership of the Writers' Guild of Great Britain means that writers need not be isolated'. Established in 1958 the Writer's Guild of Great Britain ensures that all types of writers are properly represented. They have negotiated payment terms for writers in the television, radio, theatre, cinema and publishing worlds. Basically, the site describes what it has achieved and what it continues to strive for in a variety of different writing fields. Simply click your area of interest in the blue section under the heading Departments. These links are then available from each subsequent page, at the top. Membership also brings a bi-monthly newsletter and a monthly 'work sheet' containing writing opportunities. The Guild will be of great use to a lot of writers, and this newly designed web site is professional, concise and informative.

SPECIAL FEATURES

Departments Each link under this heading tells you about the Writer's Guild's involvement in that particular field. Click the links on the left of the page to go to a variety of relevant industry sites, articles and things of interest.

About Us Find out who you're dealing with and why. Lots of links of interest too.

Join The Guild How much it costs, how to join and an illustrious list of some of the writers who are already signed up.

News Updated fairly frequently. Keeps you up to date with all the Guild news. Members give some insight into the writing profession, plus the Jargon Buster which explains industry jargon and organisations, with links to sites where appropriate, to the uninitiated. From the AAA (Association of Authors Agents) to WIPO (World Intellectual Property Organisation).

A nice looking site, doing a sterling job for British writers.

Chapter 04
miscellaneous

One of the beauties of writing is that not everything can be categorised. Anyone can write anything in an infinite number of ways. It allows the writer a wonderful freedom. However, for a guide like this it means there must always be a Miscellaneous chapter for all those sites that refused to be squeezed somewhere else.

So, here you will find yourself in the company of sites dealing with copyright, with web content, with flash fiction, with writer's block and more. There are wonderful pages to get you writing again and even a site that comes to your aid when rejection letters get you down. Most of these sites are of interest no matter what genre you might be focussed on.

www.plainenglish.co.uk
Plain English

Overall rating: ★ ★ ★ ★ ★			
Classification:	Official site	**Content:**	★ ★ ★ ★ ★
Updating:	Daily	**Readability:**	★ ★ ★ ★ ★
Navigation:	★ ★ ★ ★ ★	**Speed:**	★ ★ ★ ★ ★

UK

Plain English is described as 'language that the intended audience can understand and act upon from a single reading' and if you're writing for the public domain and you don't do so as clearly as you possibly can, you could well face the wrath of this influential organisation. They concentrate their campaign on those pieces of writing we all have to read to get through our day to day lives, so fiction writers and recreational writers can relax. Their policy towards words is also applied to their website design. All the pages are very simple and clear. The links are down the right hand side of each page and if you hover your mouse pointer over the link name, a surprisingly detailed description appears.

SPECIAL FEATURES

About The Campaign An introduction, some fascinating facts, and a detailed history of Chrissie Maher, the founder and initial driving force behind the campaign.

Free Guides A series of informative guides to using Plain English on websites, in design and layout of documents, when writing reports or letters. There's a list of alternative words to help get your message across more clearly. All the files are available on their own page and most of them are also available in PDF format for viewing on an Adobe Acrobat Reader. If you don't have the Reader, follow the link to go to Adobe's homepage where you can download one for free.

Books and Magazines A selection of books and magazines, available free or for a small charge. They include The Plain English Story, A-Z Guide to Legal Words, and Utter Drivel which lists some of the most mind-boggling statements from public documents, which makes amusing reading whilst underlining the need for the Plain English campaign.

Other Features Details of the annual awards. Training course information. Some examples of the waffle that the campaign is trying to stamp out. The use of Plain English is discussed and applied to a variety of topics, including Law, Health, Finance and Pensions. The Crystal Mark section lists organisations and institutions that have received the Plain English seal of approval for communicating clearly with the public.

Excellent campaign that deserves everyone's support.

www.contentious.com
Contentious

Overall rating: ★★★★			
Classification:	Ezine	Content:	★★★★
Updating:	Regularly	Readability:	★★★★★
Navigation:	★★★★★	Speed:	★★★★★

US

The actual online content of websites is a largely overlooked area of writing, which seems odd when the entire internet relies upon it. However, it is of great importance to visitors who will surf on to another site if the current one's content is not up to scratch. Contentious.com addresses issues concerning what you write on your site and how you present it. If you have a website, or are planning one, then you can pick up some excellent tips on how to make your content as clear as possible and make your site work for you. This a very efficiently designed site. Links are down the left of every page and everything loads super fast. Once you've applied the advice freely available here, site owner, Amy, is also available for hire to cast her expert eye over your online content, as well as a number of other services. A different slant on the usual 'writing' site, but if this is your area you'll be glad you stopped by.

SPECIAL FEATURES

Subscribe Full text or just summaries, you'll receive articles and news for free. New issues are generally monthly.

Archives See what you've been missing and get a feel of what's to come.

News Online Content news, updated every 15 minutes.

Helps you make the most of writing that will eventually end up as web content.

www.copyrightvault.com
Copyrightvault.com

Overall rating: ★★★★			
Classification:	E-commerce	Content:	★★★★
Updating:	Monthly	Readability:	★★★
Navigation:	★★★★★	Speed:	★★★★★

UK

Every writer, at some time will worry about their writing ideas being stolen. We all do it. Never mind that everything we write down is technically copyrighted to us as soon as the words are written. We always seek further reassurances. The Americans have had a service like this for a long time and this site is aimed at UK residents and Australian/New Zealand citizens. Basically, you send your writing to them, by a wide range of mediums, and Copyrightvault store everything for you. Then they send you a certificate, stating the date they took receipt of your work. In the future, if you are ever in a dispute concerning the date you wrote something, you can produce this certificate as independent evidence. They already have more than 2000 separate users accessing the site every month, but it is unclear how many of these are actually using the service. Work out the most economical way of sending in your writing, songs, even your website pages before parting with your cash. The design is economical but clear and easy to read. Pages load pretty quickly too. The navigation links are in the dark blue section, on the top left of every page.

SPECIAL FEATURES

Submit Work The all important price list and details of how to submit online or by post.

FAQ Make sure you know what you get for your money and how the whole service works.

Solicitors If you should get into legal wranglings, the site has lists of professionals, organised geographically. They all offer a ten or twenty minute first consultation for free.

Terms and conditions This link is naughtily hidden away on the Submit Work page, when really it should be available as part of the main site links. Why? Well, it's very important you read this small print. For example they don't promise that your certificate will have any legal bearing whatsoever in a court of law, or that it will be effective, at all, in doing what you hope it will do. There's also the point that if you want your material returned it will cost you a further ten pounds.

None of these are intended as criticisms of the site or the service, however, take some time to read and reread these terms before you spend your money.

Excellent for providing a little more copyright peace of mind.

---

www.eaze..net/~jfbarber/ez/creative/frameset.html
Dr. John's Eazy-Peazy Guide to Creative Writing Ideas

Overall rating: ★★★★			
Classification:	Homepage	**Content:**	★★★★
Updating:	Frequently	**Readability:**	★★★★★
Navigation:	★★★★★	**Speed:**	★★★★★

US

You've soaked up all the information offered to you by the sites in this guide. You've learnt how to set out your work like the professionals. You've found publishers, editors and film companies to approach with your finished masterpiece. Then you realise you can't think of a single thing to write. Technically you're superb, creatively you've dried up. But help is at hand from this ever-so-slightly bizarre site filled with a variety of Idea Engines to get you creatively back on track. Some of them are simple and surprisingly useful, others a little bit more cerebral. In all cases, words or sentences or whole paragraphs are randomly generated to spark off new ideas for you. If you don't like what you get, simply click again and you'll get another one. All set up by perhaps the internet's most helpful lecturer, John F. Barber, Ph. D.

This is a very simple looking site and easy to navigate using the left hand column.

SPECIAL FEATURES

Essay Engine Every time you reload the page you get a randomly generated five paragraph essay. Mostly it's gobble-de-gook, occasionally it's funny, and even more occasionally there's a real gem that gets you thinking.

Quote Engine People actually said these things. Keep clicking until one appears that inspires you to write.

Prompt Engine Odd thoughts and absurd notions like, 'If a turtle doesn't have a shell, is he homeless or naked?', to get you thinking.

Fortune Engine No need to eat a complete Chinese meal before getting these predictive snippets. These could be very useful for coming up with the core of a story.

Profundity Engine Dazzle your reader with these profound outpourings. Then just hope they don't ask you to explain them.

Names Engine Walter Nichols, Carlton Edwards, Ethel Black, Betty Kraemer. All created by the random name generator. Very useful tool that can save you lots of time wondering what your characters should be called.

Vocabulary Engine Increase your word power with these links to 'wordy' sites.

Some of these tools may seem a little daft at first, but when writer's block descends, or you're simply looking for a slice of inspiration, try them out. They might just be exactly what you need.

http://furiouspen.8m.com/
Furious Pen

Overall rating: ★ ★ ★ ★			
Classification:	Ezine	**Content:**	★ ★ ★ ★
Updating:	Quarterly	**Readability:**	★ ★ ★ ★ ★
Navigation:	★ ★ ★ ★ ★	**Speed:**	★ ★ ★ ★ ★

(PH)

Flash fiction is basically very short fiction. At this fairly new site that means anything written in less than 200 words. Sounds easy? It's actually quite a discipline in itself and is a great genre to approach when your huge novel simply refuses to flow from your fingers. This is a very simple site. Every couple of months it produces an online publication filled with flash fiction. Each issue is themed and writers can send in up to three stories at a time. For your convenience and reading pleasure, the whole issue can be downloaded as a PDF file to be viewed on Adobe's Acrobat reader. You can download this from various sites on the internet if you don't already have it. All issues are available by clicking Current Issue or Archives. The main links are in the green box at the top of the page.

SPECIAL FEATURES

Guidelines very important if you want to see your writing included in a future issue. You couldn't ask for them to be any clearer.

Download This is where you can have the PDF file downloaded onto your machine. Try it out, it makes the pages look nicer and you can read them off line at your leisure.

Subscribe Have future editions posted to your email address for free.

Well presented site for a topic that is both a genre in its own right and also a great writing exercise.

www.rejectioncollection.com
Rejection Collection.com

Overall rating: ★ ★ ★		
Classification: Homepage	**Content:**	★ ★ ★ ★
Updating: Weekly	**Readability:**	★ ★ ★ ★ ★
Navigation: ★ ★ ★ ★ ★	**Speed:**	★ ★ ★ ★

(US)

'The Writer's and Artists online source for misery, commiseration and inspiration'.

All writers know what it's like. You've finally plucked up the courage to send your work off to someone you hope will love it, use it and maybe even pay you for the privilege. Then, every day when the post arrives, you battle with a mixture of excitement and dread. Then it's there, your reply, you open it...and they don't want it. At all. Don't let it get you down, it won't be the last rejection letter you ever receive. Instead, come to Rejection Collection, spend time with equally unwanted writers. Then get your writing out to someone new. Publishers? What do they know anyway?

Get ready to laugh in the face of rejection and work off some of that negative energy that builds up when yet another unsold piece of your writing drops back through the letterbox. Everyone gets rejections, everyone. Don't worry too much about it, it's all part of the writing life.

This is a very professional looking site with nice graphics. The main links are in bright red, around the post box.

SPECIAL FEATURES

Share Your Misery this is where you start your writing therapy. Let the site know how much the writing world doesn't want you, how it chooses to break your heart and ruin your day. Or, and it is possible, if you are one of the lucky ones who has found encouragement or a happy ending through a rejection letter, then why not share it? Make sure you read the Rules of the Road first, you don't want to be rejected from here too.

Read 'em and Weep Rejection letters in nine different categories. Some pleasant and interesting or helpful, some very straight forward. At the time of writing there were close to 300 actual letters posted. For your enjoyment there are a few poems about rejection, several dozen stories by people who have more to say about their disappointments or who were rebuffed without getting letters. There are even a few postings where Editors have their say from the rejecting end of the equation. And, just so you don't get the impression this site is completely about failure, there are lots of Rewards of Rejection postings, where writers tell how rejection spurred them on to success.

Question My Authority Catherine Wald lets you know why she's qualified to be the brains behind this site.

Subscribe Have The Reject's Rag emailed to you every couple of months. It's free. And they won't turn you down. All the past issues are here for you to read.

Fun slant that takes some of the pain out of rejection.

www.sff.net/People/LisaRC/into2.htm
Get into it

Overall rating: ★★★			
Classification:	Homepage	**Content:**	★★★★
Updating:	Sporadically	**Readability:**	★★★
Navigation:	★★★★	**Speed:**	★★★★★

CAN

Other Features Decide if you are really suffering from block and why it might be happening. There's a section of some other Things That Might Help too as well as some books on the subject, which you could try to find at a British online bookseller.

Interesting to find a whole site dedicated to such a common writing problem. Any chance of a less star-filled design?

When suffering from writer's block, this site has some very useful thoughts and ideas to get you kick-started again. However, it has to be said that this is not a pleasant looking site. The writing is difficult to read and the design is not good. If you're suffering from writer's block, you may already be seeing stars of your own, but rest assured, in this case at least, the irritating stars you see in front of you are all on the site, not in your head. The dreadfully designed links are the hard to see white writing around the edge of the homepage. But ultimately, all this aside, this site is here to help you. Each page holds an independent essay on the topic of writer's block. Most of them are fairly self explanatory, and written in a rather sprawling, meandering tone. But if writer's block has you firmly by the throat, you'll be glad of assistance of any kind.

SPECIAL FEATURES

what NOT to Do Some wise thoughts about how to get through the block without being too hard on yourself.

the amazing WRITE-o-MATIC! Not really amazing, but a simple tool for getting you back on the writing trail again. Write a word, a sentence, a paragraph, write anything as a first step away from writer's block.

exercises Four fairly basic ways to get the creative juices flowing again. Just follow the instructions one by one.

OTHER SITES OF INTEREST
Copyright Licensing Agency
http://www.cla.co.uk

The home of the UK's Reproduction Rights Organisation. It looks after the interest of all those who hold rights in books, periodicals and journals. They oversee the distribution of licenses allowing organisations in Education, Business and Government to copy rights holders work. Then they ensure that monies are collected for the above copying and distributed accordingly. Also worth checking is the huge list of other copyright organisations involved with the licensed copying of every kind of work imaginable.

Funds for Writers
http://www.fundsforwriters.com/index.html

A very useful site for those writers to whom making money from their writing is the main consideration. It doesn't warrant a full page review, because much of the information is for Americans only. You won't find much here in the way of 'how to' articles. Everything is geared to cash. There are details of grants, awards and fellowships for writers. There are also some excellent articles where writers talk about ways they make money from their work, which can be applied to writers anywhere in the world. You can even choose to have updates posted to you so you won't miss out. Dig around, you never know what riches await you.

Garbl's Fat-Free-Writing Links
http://garbl.home.attbi.com/writing/concise.htm

Part of a much larger portal site filled with links to the more technical aspects of getting words down on paper in the best possible way. These links have been picked out for special mention because they cover that all too familiar writing problem of filling your work with unnecessary wordy clutter. These links take you to new places that address the most common problems, and tell you how to avoid them in future. More useful than you might imagine.

How to Get Paid Writing Simple Greeting Cards
http://morecash.moreprofits.com/1047.html

It's a single article but it carries almost as much information as some entire books on the subject. It covers a range of issues including what companies are looking for and how it's best to approach them. This is actually presented as a money-making business and even works out the money making potential. Ignore the hype, but take on board the ideas. Although American, much of the thinking applies just as well to the UK. In any case this site will get you thinking along the right lines and producing something you could sell.

Paradise
http://www.lovebytes.org.uk/paradise/

Imagine a deserted city. A thousand empty buildings waiting to be filled. This city exists online and is called Paradise. Any passing writer can wander the floor plan of it's streets. Find occupied buildings and read what the owners have chosen to write. There are no rules here, anyone can claim a plot, write something long, something short, send it in and in a couple of days the world will be able to visit your property and read your creative input. This project is funded by the Arts Council of England. Go on, get involved.

Chapter 05
non-fiction

Writers are often thought of as being either writers of fiction...or not. End of story. However, more and more novelists write articles and 'how to' books, whilst journalists, gardeners, columnists and even ex-members of parliament are turning their hands to full length fiction. Ultimately writers write. To some degree each and every one of us specialises, but no writer should close themselves off to the possibility of tackling any genre.

Many writers choose fiction because, obviously, they feel they have something to say, but also, as a beginner, it seems to be more appropriate to rattle off a short story or a few pages of a novel, in the half hours snatched for writing in an otherwise hectic day. But surely an article can be put together in much the same way, time-wise? If you're looking for something a little more personal, journal writing is coming back into fashion.

The following sites will help get you started looking for non-fiction ideas, writing them down and then marketing them. Journalists have a number of sites specifically targeted to their needs and more general sites for freelance writers offer wonderful education, encouragement and inspiration.

Couple the sites in this chapter with the excellent sites detailing publications and newspapers, in the Reference chapter and you have a world of possibilities at your fingertips.

www.freelancewriting.com
Freelance Writing

Overall rating: ★★★★			
Classification:	Community	**Content:**	★★★★★
Updating:	Fortnightly	**Readability:**	★★★★★
Navigation:	★★★★★	**Speed:**	★★★★★

(US)

Very impressive site that has so much reference material, links and features for freelance writers, that it really has to be called a community. Although the header refers to this as a site for 'working writers', you will find plenty of help and encouragement, whether you are earning your living from writing or have yet to sell your first piece. So much so that non-working writers will greatly improve their chances of changing that and start selling their work. All the pages load fairly quickly and the links for the site run attractively down the left of each and every page.

SPECIAL FEATURES

Web Events 'You are not alone' seems to be the message here, and there is always something going on you can get involved with. This is the home of the bi-weekly newsletter. There are listings of free workshops, seminars, chats with authors, and events to participate in on the internet. You can also find details of recent book deals and script deals so you can always keep up with who's doing what. If you're looking for a competition or two with cash prizes, look no further. If something a little more permanent appeals to you, there are both freelance jobs & other writing opportunities. Not bad for simply filling in your email address.

Much of the information in the newsletter is America based so check that you comply with any geographical considerations before getting carried away.

Reading Room Less of a room, more of an entire library. There are lots of sections. For the sake of your personal relationships, don't try to read everything in one sitting or you may never see the light of day again. You can subscribe to Freelancing 4 Money, a free newsletter from another web site. There are also details of how you get to read archived copies. There are excellent interviews with published authors, providing insight and encouragement. The Writers' Idea Lab is a superb resource. A question is asked and other writers visiting the site give their own thoughts. For example, a recent question asked 'What types of writing do you enjoy or do most and why?' more than fifty writers responded. There are more than 200 articles on subjects ranging from Copywriting to articles about the business side of writing. Finally there is a huge list of links for research purposes. Excellent, excellent section of the site.

Career Centre Currently there are fourteen forward links from this new page. There are a variety of jobs and numerous requests for freelancers. If you're a writer seeking work why not add your details to the dozens of others. There's a section where writers ask for help with research. A database of online talent. Unfortunately it puts the newest advertisers at the end, rather than the beginning, so it seems unlikely new posts will get much internet traffic. There's a market place, online guidelines, and soon there will even be links to other job sites. Phew.

Networking Centre 28 writing forums, some barely used. They vary from Technical Writing to Copywriting, Magazine writing, and a main lobby where anything related to writing can be aired.

Every writing site should have to be this impressive. There should be a law.

www.journalismuk.co.uk
Journalism UK

Overall rating: ★ ★ ★ ★			
Classification:	Portal	Content:	★ ★ ★ ★ ★
Updating:	Weekly	Readability:	★ ★ ★ ★ ★
Navigation:	★ ★ ★ ★ ★	Speed:	★ ★ ★ ★ ★

UK

Essentially, the 'one journalist and one techie' who maintain this site simply wanted to collect together links that the professional journalist might find of value. This they have done and this rather attractive site is the result. What they didn't bank on was lots and lots of people getting in touch with them about vague or irrelevant topics, many having nothing at all to do with journalism. Their thoughts on these people and the questions they ask is dealt with in the FAQ, which makes them essential and often amusing reading. The navigation couldn't be easier. Everything you need is in the column on the left and could probably do with being just a little bit bigger for the sake of your eyes. You'll soon see that these links don't take you to individual new pages but to the relevant part of a big long page containing everything else on the site. We like it, as it provides quick loading information.

SPECIAL FEATURES

Magazines Comprehensive list of magazine publishers or sites that catalogue magazine sites. If you can't find the title you want at the first link there are more than twenty others to try. Wonderful resource.

News Sources If you want to know what's going on in the world there are more than thirty links to local, British and International News sites. If you can't find reference to a particular news story here, it obviously didn't happen.

Organisations Useful links to everything from the Campaign Against Censorship of the Internet in Britain, to several Find an Expert sites.

OTHER FEATURES

Links to all the national papers and directories of hundreds of local newspapers. Small selection of ezine links. Lots of links to training courses and all-important job sites for journalists. International links. Science, Sport and Entertainment sites are also featured.

A fantastic one-stop resource for journalists and freelancers alike.

www.writingthejourney.com
Writing the Journey – Online Journal Writing Workshop

Overall rating: ★★★★		
Classification: Workshop	**Content:**	★★★★
Updating: Occasionally	**Readability:**	★★★★★
Navigation: ★★★★★	**Speed:**	★★★★★

(US)

Writing a journal or a diary is perhaps one of the first ways a person starts their writing life. One of the beauties of the genre is that it cannot be wrong. There are no rules regarding structure, no industry codes about presentation. There is simply the writer and his/her innermost thoughts and experiences. In many cases the words are written without ever expecting, or wanting, anyone else to read them. Often the writer has no intention of even re-reading the journal, writing simply for the joy or cathartic properties of their outpouring. But, even if none of these reasons apply to you, keeping a diary or journal is an excellent way to keep you writing, keep the words tumbling out of you and being recorded. This site has a clean and fresh design that is instantly appealing. It's user friendly both in navigation and tone and is a wonderful place for all writers currently working on, or thinking of, writing a journal.

There are links all over the home page, as red words in the body of the page; on the small notebook at the top on the left; and there are further links don the right hand side too.

SPECIAL FEATURES

First Visit The obvious starting point. Find out what's going on here and how to easily access some of the most popular sections of the site.

Returning Nicely designed, so that many of the questions you might have when returning to the site, are laid out for you to click. For example, 'I want to do your exercises offline' or 'I want to see a list of everything on your site'. This information is all available elsewhere, but the simplicity of the design is a nice touch.

Workshop The heart of the site. Read the basics of journal writing, use some thought provoking exercises to ensure you get the most out of your journal writing experience; and check out the few articles covering journals in greater depth.

Organize! Like any type of writing, one of the hardest obstacles to overcome is our very own inability to organise our writing into our busy schedules. This section tackles exactly this problem.

Goodies Free Software, Printable Exercises, and more.

OTHER FEATURES

Don't forget to sign up for the free monthly newsletter. All that's required is your email address. However, at the time of writing the Newsletter has ground to a halt, but the Resources link on the home page allows you to look at lots of past issues, which have masses of interesting stuff, as well as some suggested reading.

Everything you could need to get you started and keep you writing a journal.

www.gn.apc.org/media/nuj.html
National Union of Journalists

Overall rating: ★★★★			
Classification:	Trade Union	**Content:**	★★★★
Updating:	Fortnightly	**Readability:**	★★★★
Navigation:	★★★★	**Speed:**	★★★★★

(UK)

30,000 members make this the largest journalists' union in the world. The site is unofficial, although it is maintained by the London freelance Branch of the NUJ. The official site, when it's up and running will be found at http://www.nuj.org.uk.

It's a very simple looking site and wouldn't win any design awards but it does load quickly and navigation is fairly straightforward. The site is split into three sections, each containing links to further content. Under the heading Update you can find links to the most recent industry news and issues. The Online Departments are more permanent sections of information and includes details of how to join the NUJ, and there is also a useful Oft-visited pages section, the best of these are covered below. Many of the pages have links within them, to keep you moving until you find exactly what you're looking for.

SPECIAL FEATURES

Advice & Tuition Details of how to connect to the internet abroad, how to deal with virus' and other computer related help. You will also find Copyright and Contracts information so you know exactly where you stand. On the legal front, there's a list of Journalism courses, and further advice and contacts.

Media sites & resources Links to news services, newspapers and periodicals from around the world. There are also links to Governmental and political bodies. The Resources section at the top of the page has lots of further reading.

Guide to Copyright Essential information about one of writing's most troublesome areas.

OTHER FEATURES

Contacts, branches, links & directories Need to find an address or a contact a branch of the Union? Then this should be your first stop.

NUJ policies, papers & campaigns Nitty-gritty about the campaigns the union has been fighting, issues they've been raising. There are a selection of documents and articles relating to policy that can be read online.

A useful site for Journalists and Freelancers alike.

www.yudkin.com/publish.htm
Published! How to Reach Writing Success

Overall rating: ★★★★		
Classification: Guide	**Content:**	★★★★
Updating: Monthly	**Readability:**	★★★★★
Navigation: ★★★★★	**Speed:**	★★★★★

US

Writers are lucky, the internet provides many, many talented writers willing to offer you advice and help you on the way to a bigger and better writing career. The talent here is Marcia Yudkin. She has published ten of her own books and hundreds of articles. She also teaches writing through both seminars and courses, so you could say she knows her stuff. Her simple, yet informative site is filled with articles to help your writing. She also advertises her home learning course, and her work as a Writing Coach. Obviously, both these options will cost you money, but you do get personal attention, which can be invaluable.

The articles run, simply, down the homepage, while the site links are on the left. There are no 'let's be trendy' graphics or backgrounds, so the whole site loads really quickly, which is another reason we like it.

SPECIAL FEATURES

Free Articles & Resources No need to click a link to get to these. Everything is there already on the homepage, with the most recent articles at the top of the page. The articles cover all sorts of writing topics and include resources, finding markets, working with editors, publicity, manuscript submission and much more. There is a particularly good link for help with the Marketing and Publicity of your web site.

Breaking into Major Magazines This is where all the nitty-gritty of the home study course is laid out. It should be noted that the course assumes that you are at least familiar with the basics of article writing. This one is not for absolute beginners.

Audiotapes & Books by Marcia Yudkin There are a wealth of titles on sale, covering all kinds of writing lessons and advice. They can be purchased online using a credit card, and the server is secure, so you can buy with confidence.

Other Features A free newsletter offers you a minute's worth of marketing advice. It's free and comes every Wednesday. Details of Marcia's Writing Coach service and her Earn $100/Hour with your Writing Skills course are also available. However, as there is a great deal of faxing information back and forth you will, obviously, need a 24 hour access to a fax machine. Marcia would also prefer her students were North America based.

Great articles almost make up for the fact that you really should be in the US to get the absolute best of her expertise.

www.worldwidefreelance.com
Worldwide Freelance Writers

Overall rating: ★ ★ ★		
Classification: Guide	**Content:**	★ ★ ★ ★
Updating: Bi-weekly	**Readability:**	★ ★ ★ ★ ★
Navigation: ★ ★ ★ ★ ★	**Speed:**	★ ★ ★ ★ ★
(HK)		

An attractive site, providing freelance writers with a range of useful information. The main selling point is the section on markets. From a variety of categories you can read the actual writer's guidelines from a growing list of publications. But this site aims to be more than just a list of links. To give it more substance the site also has a collection of articles for the freelancer as well as recommending a variety of books, all of which are linked to the American version of Amazon. In order to stay ahead of the crowd why not sign up for the free newsletter filled with market and writing news. It's also worth mentioning that the site is a paying market itself. See below for details.

The site is very easy to navigate using the buttons on the left of every page.

SPECIAL FEATURES

Markets Choose the continent you're interested in and very quickly you are presented with the complete list of titles. Each title has full submission guidelines and contact details. On the Markets page you will find all the newest editions on the right hand side. It's also worth checking out the Special market Report which includes 50 Travel Writing Markets and 70 Computer and IT Markets.

Articles Writers with a decidedly international flavour share their thoughts with this range of excellent articles. At the bottom of the page is a link for those writers wishing to write for the site.

Free Newsletter You will no doubt have already seen the pop-up screen inviting you to subscribe to the newsletter. It comes up every single time you click the Markets button. Very annoying. This is the more civilised way to sign up. Read a sample copy to see what's in store.

Other Features A search engine allows you to search the whole site for a key word and then delivers the results with a somewhat arbitrary 'score'. There is also a fairly good links section.

Not the biggest market list on the internet but intelligent articles and newsletter make it a very useful site.

www.writershome.com		
The Writers Home		
Overall rating: ★★★★		
Classification: Guide	**Content:**	★★★★
Updating: Occasionally	**Readability:**	★★★★
Navigation: ★★★★★	**Speed:**	★★★★★
US		

This site for freelance writers has a sense of fun stamped all over it. There are cartoons and funny little bits and pieces all over the site. The Homepage immediately gives a feel of what's in store. Three bright bands of colour, a comedy bookworm, and witty fillers abound. However, some people might find this approach a little laid back, casual even. Does the site actually look, in a certain light, like a site for children? Maybe. But the content is good and a sense of fun and lack of stress never hurt anyone. So get reading.

It's a good site for writers of articles and other non-fiction, editors, and for those who want to chill out when the pressures of writing loom large. Navigate using the links down the left of the Homepage. These are down the right side of subsequent pages.

SPECIAL FEATURES

Instruction This is the good stuff. Really easy to navigate sections on all aspects of non-fiction writing. Everything from finding ideas, writing them down and eventually selling them. Excellent, calmly written, solid advice that's easy to read, supportive and gives you confidence. You don't want to type a single word until these pages have been thoroughly digested. They will make the whole writing process much easier.

Article Ideas To get the creativity flowing, the guys who run this site chat about how they find their own ideas and provide links down the right of the section, taking you to specific areas of interest.

Humour Pages Writing can be hard work when you're staring at a blank page and your mind is lacking all intelligent thought. Don't be too hard on yourself. Poke around this large humour section, give yourself a laugh and a break. Ms Muse will be back in no time. Scroll down the page for all the different humour sections they cover.

On Books Book reviews, interviews with writers, links to top writers' web sites and loads of links to publishers' web sites. Good for reference.

OTHER FEATURES

Your Resume $24 to have a link to your site and a fifty word description of your talents pasted into the Editors Only section of The Writers Home for a year.

Editors Only This is where the writing resumes live. There are also links to things of interest for Editors, both on this site and around the internet. Editors also get a link to their very own humour section.

Great site for article writers, especially if you're a little stuck for ideas.

www.youcanwrite.com
You Can Write

Overall rating: ★★★★		
Classification: Guide	**Content:**	★★★★
Updating: Occasionally	**Readability:**	★★★★★
Navigation: ★★★★★	**Speed:**	★★★★★

(US)

Instead of taking you by the hand and carefully walking you through the trials and tribulations of finding non-fiction ideas and writing them down in the best order, You Can Write sits you down in it's office, looks you straight in the eye and tells you how it is. They treat writing seriously because it is. It's a business, it's about selling a product and they know all about this. They just want to make sure you know it too. Don't let this no-nonsense approach put you off, if you're serious about writing and then selling what you write, you will find this site invaluable.

Most of the information is expanded upon in a series of Insider Guides, which you can purchase and download as ebooks. This is one of the prime reasons for the site being here at all. They give you some really good 'Free Stuff' to grab your attention and encourage you to go further and make a purchase. The guides are all fairly reasonably priced in US dollars, but as their quality is the same as the site, the guides are excellent and your money is well spent. Use the links with the blue dots on the left of the screen to navigate.

SPECIAL FEATURES

Publishing A short discussion on the state of publishing and you as a potential writer in that business.

Book Proposals Publishers give some thoughts on what they want and how best to impress them. Very useful to know.

Agents Want to catch their attention? Don't sit on their doorstep or phone them every five minutes. Try these ten more practical ways instead.

Writing Industry professionals share some of their experience and words of wisdom. Again, it's extremely important to listen to those in the know.

Writers Resources Long list of books and sites you might find helpful. There is very little description of what to expect and the books could do with links to places to buy them online. As always we recommend searching for the books on UK book sites.

A site that reminds you that writing something good is only half the battle to seeing it published.

www.ioj.co.uk
The Chartered Institute of Journalists

Overall rating: ★★★

Classification:	Official site	Content:	★★★
Updating:	Occasionally	Readability:	★★★★★
Navigation:	★★★★★	Speed:	★★★★

UK

The world's oldest organisation for Journalists, the CIoJ is both a professional organisation and a Trade Union, representing and protecting the interests of its members. Basically this site wants you to join its ranks, and as a journalist, you might find it in your best interest to do just that. Navigation of the site couldn't be simpler, all the links are at the bottom of each page, click the bright red CIoJ buttons to go to your area of choice. It's a little sluggish at times, but the pages are clear and easy to read. There isn't a great deal at the site, but as a journalist you may find membership valuable. Check out their History, what they do now and how membership can benefit you.

SPECIAL FEATURES

On-line Membership Application For your convenience you can apply for membership online. There are four levels of membership depending on your job and professional experience. The forms are very clear, as are the payment details. Upon filling out the form online you will be asked to choose which subscription rate applies to you, but will not be asked to give any credit card details at this point.

Institute Journals The last two issues in full. They're quite big downloads (more than a Mb) and you'll also need an Acrobat Reader to view the files. There's no link to the software here, but it is freely available elsewhere on the internet.

Useful organisation, although their site could do with more content.

OTHER SITES OF INTEREST

Journalist Express
http://www.journalistexpress.com/

A mammoth collection of links for journalists. Although aimed squarely at journalists across the pond, any one can take advantage of the free membership. Just fill in your personal details. You will then be able to customise which links you see and which are of no interest. You'll find links to many newspapers and magazines, stock markets, broadcast news, gossip, reference sites, statistics, people searches, directories, do we need to go on. Huge potential for keeping up with the news and also finding information to research your own writing or even inspire you to come up with fresh news stories.

The Nonfiction Writers Workshop
http://www.manistee.com/~lkraus/workshop/nfiction.html

Part of the Internet Writing Workshop but worth mentioning in it's own right simply because it gives a forum where magazine articles, essays and even book length non-fiction works are posted and critiques invited. Participation is the only membership criteria, so don't expect to post your work without reading the work of others. Membership is free. A great site for feedback and for polishing all your non-fiction writing. Recent technical problems with dead links on the homepage are now a thing of the past.

Chapter 06

prose

The one type of writing to which, on the whole, there are no constraints. Your writing might be a short story of a few hundred words or a huge historical sage of several hundred thousand words. There are no rules about themes, or characters, or subject matter. Every genre has sub-genres and there's still room for anything brand new you might come up with. There are still hugely popular niche markets for every subject imaginable: Romance, Spying, Thriller, Erotica, Humour, War, Westerns, Horror, Science Fiction etc. You can just as easily pick any two genres from the above list, combine them and find a smaller, but equally keen target market.

The websites that follow include a broad range of subject matter. There are 'how to' sites on a variety of genres, and critique sites that will help you hone your writing skills. Others carry more general advice on structure, tone, characters and all the other facets of a story that you'll need to create a good, strong, successful piece of prose writing.

No form of writing is easy, but these sites will help you stop thinking it's impossible.

www.critters.org
Critters Workshop

Overall rating: ★ ★ ★ ★			
Classification:	Critique group	Content:	★ ★ ★ ★ ★
Updating:	Weekly	Readability:	★ ★ ★ ★ ★
Navigation:	★ ★ ★ ★ ★	Speed:	★ ★ ★ ★ ★

(US)

More than three thousand members have written over 90,000 critiques of each other's Science Fiction, Fantasy, and Horror fiction. Antarctica is the only continent yet to get involved, members from the other six are already getting stuck in. This is how it works. You send your writing to the group. It goes in a queuing system and you wait until it's your turn and it is sent out to the membership, along with a couple of dozen of other pieces. Then you wait. Most people get between 15 and 20 critiques of their work. Just stop for a moment and think how invaluable that would be to you as a writer. Exactly. So join.

The only requirement of membership is that you participate. On average you need to critique one piece of work a week. The workshop has very strict guidelines about participating and you will not have your work sent out if you're not joining in. For further information, work your way down the main page for the various red-dotted sections.

What this site does is superb. Most importantly, it will help your writing to improve.

SPECIAL FEATURES

Want to know more? Click the various links to find out in more detail exactly how it works and what to expect. On pain of death, don't forget to check the Rules and Format Guidelines. Or people will get cross.

Want to join? Here's where you sign up. It's free.

Need resources on critiquing, writing or SF? If you're going to receive critiques, you'll want them to be as useful as possible. Make sure the critiques you write are up to scratch by clicking on these links on how to write a great critique and links to market info and writer's resources.

Who are we? Huge list of the members of the group. Hopefully, before too long many of them will be reading your work and telling you what they think of your writing.

What's in the queue? This will give you some idea of the enormity of what's going on here. A complete list of what's coming up as well as details of every piece of writing that's been submitted over the years, including title, genre and the writer's name.

If this is your genre and you want to know what other writers think, this will be a home from home.

www.horror.org
Horror Writers Association

Overall rating: ★★★★		
Classification: Association	**Content:**	★★★★★
Updating: Fortnightly	**Readability:**	★★★★★
Navigation: ★★★★★	**Speed:**	★★★★★
US		

Horror and Dark Fantasy authors have this excellent organisation to promote their interests. There were some pretty heavyweight writers involved at its conception during the 80s, including Dean Koontz and Robert McCammon. They have great resources, encourage networking and have some real clout in the industry. Editors have said that membership of the association shows a writer is professional and serious about his writing. Members reside all over the world. You don't have to be a published writer in the genre, you simply have to have a 'significant interest in Horror and dark Fantasy', to become an associate member. Active members must have published some of their writings. The site recommends the UK chapter of the society, but at the time of writing it had sadly closed down.

This is a supremely professional site, both in design and attitude. It costs to join, but currently is a very reasonable $55 if you live in America, $65 to everyone else.

Navigate via the links on the left of each page.

SPECIAL FEATURES

About HWA A quick perusal of the page will convince you, if you still needed convincing, that this is a well organised, intelligent body who are serious about what they do and what they write. Make sure you check out the membership details and various fees. Many writing 'associations' are run by fans and keen amateurs, this one has 'professional' stamped all over it.

Application You know you want to join. Step by step, simple to follow guidelines to become a member. Unusually, although online payments are accepted, the transaction will not take place over a secure server, and therefore there is a small chance your details might be seen by unscrupulous types. However, paying by post is simple, and safe.

Writing Tips Small selection of articles on writing. Much larger list of links to other sites of interest.

HWA News Book signings, workshops, publishing information and any other relevant news, mostly sent in by the membership. All the most recently published genre books are listed here too.

Members Only Once a member, you'll get market listings, a very busy message board, industry news, a directory of agents and more. If you're not a member, you have to make do without any of them.

Stoker Awards Every year these respected awards are given for 'superior achievement' in the genre. Find out more here.

Member Pages Huge list of Message Boards, Newsgroups, Newsletters and Mailing lists, as well as dozens of member sites, including some very famous names.

Horror Links Impressive list of links to Horror News, Conventions, General Interest, Magazines (both online and off), Publishers, Booksellers, TV Networks, Film companies and a few celebrity listings. If you can't find loads here to interest you, there's something very wrong.

All writers of this genre should join in order to get the full benefit of the site.

http://literary-liaisons.com/
Literary Liaisons

Overall rating: ★★★★			
Classification:	Guide	Content:	★★★★★
Updating:	Daily	Readability:	★★★★★
Navigation:	★★★★★	Speed:	★★★★★

US

A wonderful home for historical romances. This pleasantly designed site hopes to provide something not only for the writers of this genre but also those who like to read it. You know who you are. On the opening page you'll find a list of historical occurrences. Births, firsts and interesting facts of the day. You'll find details of a good selection of genre specific books, both novels and non-fiction. Some of the book titles link to the American version of Amazon, where you can buy them. There is also a new section listing videos of interest, especially for researching a particular historical period. These too link to Amazon.com. As always, if the USA isn't your home, search for them on more local sites. The site links run down the left of the page.

SPECIAL FEATURES

Literary Liaisons Newsletter An excellent bi-monthly newsletter. Each instalment has a featured article, details of updates to the site and a fascinating calendar of event for a specific year. Archives include every past copy and these, plus registering to have future editions emailed to you, is completely free. Which can't be bad.

Research Articles For your convenience, all the articles from the newsletter are collected here, and presented in a slightly more eye-friendly manner.

Researching the Romance A huge list of print books to help you put authentic background into your stories. In order to make buying these books easier they have some or all, of the following information: title, author, publisher, publishing date and ISBN number.

Writers' Resources Online Absolutely superb list of links. There are masses and masses of information to be had here. From Fashion to Medical sections and including links as diverse as Mountain Tea Inn's Tea Room and Glossary of Old Diseases. Add to these, links to online publishers and publications, Societies and loads of general writing links, you have a very formidable library of information little more than a click away.

Other Features A Guestbook. Details of the Romance Writers of America and there huge number of online chapters, all obviously in America.

A very popular genre, more than adequately supported by this informative site.

www.stephaniebond.com
Stephanie Bond How-To Articles

Overall rating: ★ ★ ★ ★			
Classification:	Homepage	Content:	★ ★ ★ ★ ★
Updating:	Monthly	Readability:	★ ★ ★ ★ ★
Navigation:	★ ★ ★ ★ ★	Speed:	★ ★ ★ ★

US

Originally this review was only going to contain details of the Writer's Pages section of this site, but there is something about Stephanie's outlook and the way she writes on the site that is instantly both charming and engrossing. It makes the whole site appealing. She is an award winning author, best known for writing romantic comedies. The site is efficiently designed and the pages, generally, quick to load. It has been set up so Stephanie can promote her books, which is understandable, lots of writers do it. But she has also filled the site with lots of useful and entertaining bits and pieces for writers who want to be better writers. And there is no hard sell which can put you off other author sites. Navigate using the brown boxes just under the homepage header.

SPECIAL FEATURES

Writers Pages A brief question and answer session deals with some of the most common writing worries. The real gem of the site, for writers, is the library of how-to articles written by Stephanie. More than thirty articles deal with writing skills and the business of writing. A new article is added each month.

About Stephanie Interesting interview that highlights the fact that it's never too late to take up writing, no matter what other career plans you've set yourself.

Stephanie's Books Only a handful are available on the UK version of Amazon, but for writers there is extra interest in this section than simply buying books. Each title can be clicked. Each book's own page has a short but interesting 'Story Behind the Story' feature at the bottom. They discuss a little bit about where the idea for the plot came from and any other writing insight the author thinks appropriate. There are excerpts from the books too. Maybe it's because they're out of context, but passages like this seem to teach more about what published writing looks like, than an actual book does. So read and learn.

A Day in the Life Funny and insightful. Spend a day with a real professional writer, who's also a real professional person.

The Making of a Book Find out what happens after the writer has finished and delivered the manuscript. Editorial process and book design are chatted about.

Booksellers Pages Read the series of articles Stephanie wrote for booksellers containing masses of information about promotion and, well, selling books. Broadly interesting for writers too.

Informative, educational, and fun. Who could ask for more?

www.mninter.net/~emmah
Emma Holly – Erotica & Romance

Overall rating: ★★★★			
Classification:	Homepage	**Content:**	★★★★
Updating:	Twice yearly	**Readability:**	★★★★★
Navigation:	★★★★★	**Speed:**	★★★★★

(US)

Emma Holly is the author of a variety of works of fiction. A number of these have been published by Black Lace, the well known women's erotica publisher. Although predominantly used to promote her own work, this homepage offers a lot for the prospective writer of erotica. If this is the genre you want to work in, you'll find that serious erotica writing is not a very common subject on writing sites. You'll be very glad you found this one. First click on the Enter Site, after 'agreeing that you are of appropriate age and temperament to view adult material'. It's a very simple design, everything is easy to find, and the pages come quickly to your browser.

SPECIAL FEATURES

Books Emma's published works. Each title has an excerpt available which, in itself is a great lesson on how to write an erotic scene.

Workshop Without a doubt, for writer's this is the highlight of the site. A whole workshop for writers of erotica. From Overcoming Inhibitions to a point by point breakdown of a sex scene. Very intelligently written and of great help to anyone interested in writing for this genre. Also, all this excellent insight and expertise won't cost you a thing.

Other Features Links to recommended erotica sites, a little more detail about Emma, recommended reading of both erotica related titles and general Plain Old Good Reads. There are also links to buy Emma's books. Very sensibly, other sites take note, there are links for both the American and UK Amazon sites.

Goes a long way both encouraging erotica writers and breaking down inhibitions.

www.katyterrega.com/writers.html
Katy Terrega

Overall rating: ★ ★ ★ ★			
Classification: Guide/Ecommerce		**Content:** ★ ★ ★	
Updating: Bi-weekly		**Readability:** ★ ★ ★ ★ ★	
Navigation: ★ ★ ★ ★ ★		**Speed:** ★ ★ ★ ★ ★	

US

A site for that least discussed area of saleable writing: Porn. Katy Terrega, as well as being a confessed writer of porn is also a home-worker and mother. If you don't like 'adult material', get offended easily by sexual references, fantasies and the steamier side of life, don't go here. Katy, herself, says she doesn't really advertise to more than a select few, what her chosen writing path is, so writers who have similar reservations will at least find a safe haven to explore the genre. The site goes a long way towards dispelling the myth that porn/erotica is only written, and read, by the clichéd 'dirty old men' or smutty adolescents. There are some snippets of erotic writing which try to entice you into purchasing the full stories, available as ebooks. They are relatively inexpensive and can be ordered via a secure server. She has also written a number of ebook guides to the genre, which you can also buy online.

Classy looking site keeps the smut in the writing, rather than in the design. Links are on the left of the homepage.

SPECIAL FEATURES

Free Newsletter A frank, informative and friendly newsletter. It's bi-weekly and every issue contains articles, advice and information on markets. There are also Links, recommended books, a short story competition and Articles. Clicking Story Site takes you to a dedicated porn/erotica site with extremely adult links, definitely not for the young or easily offended.

An useful site for this undeniably taboo genre.

www.nicestories.com
NiceStories.com

Overall rating: ★ ★ ★ ★			
Classification: Free E-publisher		**Content:** ★ ★ ★ ★	
Updating: Daily		**Readability:** ★ ★ ★ ★ ★	
Navigation: ★ ★ ★ ★ ★		**Speed:** ★ ★ ★ ★ ★	

NL

Very simply, NiceStories.com allows you to post your stories onto the site. For free. You have to become a member, which is also totally free. All members can rate the stories they read and give feedback when they choose to. From the front page you'll see that the site is split into two sections, Standard Stories, with more than a thousand submissions, and the Stories for Young people which currently only has a few dozen stories. After clicking your choice, the basic links for the site appear in green. This is a pleasantly designed site which has an inspired option of changing the font it can be viewed in, aiding easy reading. If you want to see your work up on the internet, and don't want to pay for it, this is the place for you.

SPECIAL FEATURES

Settings Font too small? Change it here and prevent eye strain. The site must be applauded for this excellent design feature. They want you to read lots, so make it easier to do just that. There's nothing like a monitor induced headache for making you give a site a wide berth. You can also change your account details.

Author Tools Everything you need to know to get your writing on the site.

Categories See what has already been posted, in easy to find genre categories.

Other Features A fairly active message board, a comprehensive list of every author featured on the site, lists of the top rated stories and the newest submissions, and a small links page.

Possibly one of the easiest places to see your work published on the net.

www.underdown.org
The Purple Crayon

Overall rating: ★★★★			
Classification:	Guide	**Content:**	★★★★
Updating:	Monthly	**Readability:**	★★★★★
Navigation:	★★★★★	**Speed:**	★★★★★

US

This is the Homepage of an American editor of Children's books. He offers a variety of articles for writers and illustrators. He has also gathered together links of interest to all 'children's book people'. The site contains a mountain of information, and although it's aimed at American writers across the pond, much of the content is simply about good writing, which applies to everyone, no matter what accent it's written in.

The navigation links are all written in purple crayon and are all available from the homepage. Further browsing can be done by clicking the relevant parts of the purple crayon at the bottom of each subsequent page. Harold D. Underdown, whose baby this site is, makes no bones about the fact that the content of the site, especially the links, is based on what he has found useful or interesting.

Articles From the absolute basics, to writing for specific genres and interviews with industry professionals. There are also lots of articles discussing the business side of writing for children, but these are all very heavily US biased. At the bottom of this page are links to articles and sites that contain further useful articles.

Children's Great links for children's writers. There are recommended starting points as well as a whole list of specific sites for writers and illustrators.

Publishing Sites listing publishers and resources live here. As do book reviews and a slightly muddled collection of other links to editing, free fonts and examples of online publishing.

Pictures Contains links to sites providing pictures and photographs; category specific libraries and a whole series of sites dealing with maps.

Reference Excellent range of sites. Search engines are examined in depth and 15 of them are linked to. There are lots more links for finding just about anything.

Writing children's books is laid bare. However, the site has very useful content for a wider range of writers.

http://romance-central.com/index1.shtml
Romance Central

Overall rating: ★ ★ ★ ★			
Classification:	Homepage	Content:	★ ★ ★ ★
Updating:	Monthly	Readability:	★ ★ ★ ★
Navigation:	★ ★ ★ ★ ★	Speed:	★ ★ ★ ★ ★

(US)

First things first, there are lots and lots of hearts. But what did you expect, it is Romance Central. There's an awful lot going on at this site, including links which have little to do with romance and writing. So, by all means peruse the site fully, but the writing stuff is pretty much all contained under the link Writer's Workshop, which would be the obvious starting place for writers. Main links are across the top of the homepage, while down the left you will find everything the site has to offer.

SPECIAL FEATURES

Writer's Workshop Basically, this is simply a collection of articles, collected from around the web. Many of them are romance-specific, others could apply to any style of writing. Everything is organised into easy to find sections. So, if you're looking for help with Characters or Research, you can go to the specific section without having to wade through lots and lots of articles you're not interested in.

Ye Old Links Lots of links, including a huge list of, not surprisingly, Romance Links.

Message Board Fairly busy, friendly forum for all writing romance issues and more.

Lots of help for the romance writer.

www.stories.com
Stories.com

Overall rating: ★★★★			
Classification:	Community	Content:	★★★★
Updating:	Constantly	Readability:	★★★★★
Navigation:	★★★	Speed:	★★★★★

(US)

Mammoth site with almost 50,000 registered members and nearly a quarter of a million items online. We're talking big, and it's going to get bigger as some time in the future they intend to offer the site in other languages too. It's a place writers come to get help and advice from other members; post their work for others to read in their personal online portfolio; join in with an interactive story or simply to pass some time reading the many current threads in the Message Forums. The thousands of stories can be searched for by a variety of genres, which means it is possible to find like minded writers and even communicate with them by email.

Once a member, you will receive your very own URL so you can send people to your work really easily. As with any site of this magnitude, navigation can be a little tricky. The site does everything it can to point you in the right direction, but a little browsing of your own will be needed to make the most of everything on offer. There are round icons at the top of the page, hover your mouse over them to see what they stand for. There are drop down boxes to help you navigate and also links as words under the round icons. Confusing? Yea, a little.

SPECIAL FEATURES

Getting Started There's so much going on, you'll be glad that they don't mind explaining it to you.

Register Now! To get the most out of the site you have to register. It's free and doesn't ask any difficult or probing questions, so what are you waiting for?

Help Make this your next stop. Find out what's going on here, and how you can do it too.

Featured Items Read some of the best stories on the site, as voted by members. You can add authors to your Favourite Authors list for future reference.

Campfire Creatives Start a story, invite others to pick it up where you leave off. See where multiple writers can take the plot. Some writers have used these campfires to start little forums of their own. They're your campfires, so be creative.

Madlibs Add your own words to create ridiculous stories. A short amusing distraction.

Message Forums Lots of them. Get reviewed, make comments of your own or just read what's going on.

Write them, read them, rate them. Great community based on 'doing' rather than 'talking about doing'.

www.write4kids.com/index.html
Write4Kids.com

Overall rating: ★★★★			
Classification:	Guide/Ecommerce	Content:	★★★★
Updating:	Weekly	Readability:	★★★★
Navigation:	★★★	Speed:	★★★★★

(US)

Maybe it's just us, but there's something slightly irritating about a site that 'proclaims' everything, promises you success and insider information through an all encompassing sugary sweet smile. You know the sort of thing, almost every sentence ends with an exclamation mark! Very cheesy. It's obviously used as a selling ploy here because at it's heart, this site wants you to buy things from it. Books and ebooks, no doubt filled with useful information to improve your writing. Which is fine, but less cheese please.

Don't let the tone of the site put you off. If the books they are selling are as good as the free information available here, you won't be wasting your money. They manage 35,000 visitors a month which speaks volumes.

Navigation is not very straightforward, but again, this seems to be so that the adverts for their products can come up again and again in a number of different guises. You'll see what we mean as soon as you start clicking around the blue underlined wording on the homepage, or the blue navigation bar that appears on all subsequent pages, right at the top.

SPECIAL FEATURES

Begin If you're just starting out this should be your first stop. There's an introduction to the company, a link to some good advice for beginners, the first of many adverts for Career Start which you can get for $20 (US) or download a demo for nothing. The demo has lots of great information, but certain sections are disabled.

Learn Loads of How To information. Articles covering just about everything you could dream of, to do with writing for children.

Writers Resources Sign up for the free ezine, like 25,000 others have already done.

Free Stuff There's also a free messageboard which is busy but informative. There's also a very interesting news section, with mostly American items. Apparently it is considered the top forum for children's writers.

Tools 4 Success More information about the books and guides they are trying to get you to buy.

Other Features There are useful, ongoing Q&A pages, Links, and you can even search a list of writing events in your area, which is only really useful if you're in America.

A good starting point for those looking for free advice with a variety of products for those with money to spend.

OTHER SITES OF INTEREST

Cheat Sheets
http://www.michellejerott.com/cheatsheets.html

Very simply presented crib sheets for writers. There are lists to aid plotting, including Polti's 36 Dramatic Situations; Classic Romance Plots and information on 'Pitching a Book'. There is also a helpful list of often misused and abused words you should check your work for before considering it finished. Very helpful.

Crime Time
http://www.crimetime.co.uk/

Mystery and suspense author, Ed Gorman claims that this is 'The best crime magazine in the world'. Praise indeed. For the potential crime writer, or established for that matter, it's important to keep up with all that's new in the genre. You will find reviews of books, interviews with authors and a range of features about crime writing. This site has little in the way of 'how to' and is more concerned with the finished project than how a writer gets there. However, if this is your genre, you'll learn by simply immersing yourself in the site. The magazine is also available in paper form and a year's subscription will currently cost you £20.

Crime Writer's Association
http://www.thecwa.co.uk/index.html

To join you will have had a full length novel or non fiction book, a professional play, a feature film, or a number of other professional writings published. They're quite exclusive. Even if you don't fit the membership criteria, make sure you still enter the annual Debut Dagger competition, many winners go on to become published authors. If you want a member to come and talk to your organisation or group, check out the Speakers section. The Events link lists conventions in both Britain and America.

Mystery Vault.net
http://www.mysteryvault.net/

A portal site to online digests and newsletters dedicated to the ever popular Mystery genre. Each of the digests can be accessed in a number of different ways and are fully searchable for keywords. Have a wander round, there are masses of archives to explore. The top links take you from this site to the archives of the relevant list. Further down the page is more of the same, but the archives are kept on different sites, which really doesn't make much difference as you surf. All the lists are filled with people talking about mystery writing, books and associated issues. Some of these are very busy lists, so be warned, if you join up you may get masses of posts.

Chapter 07
reference

Much of your writing will come from within. You will have that 'great idea', you'll apply your own personal experience to the idea and 'write about what you know'. But then you'll need your hero to dispose of a body, fire a gun, move to another country, go back in time or do something else that is completely outside your world of experience. You'll need help. More importantly, you'll need to make sure you get your facts straight. Make a mistake and someone will notice it. Maybe lots will. Maybe your Editor will. It does not put you in a good light.

The sites in this chapter provide information and facts.

There is no excuse for making glaring mistakes. No one said that research was easy, but it will give great depth to your work if you do it properly. Research can also give you wonderful ideas for where your writing might go. It will also give you lots more ideas for further writing.

Some of the sites are very specific, to a single area of expertise, like the Police or firearms and their use. Other sites offer more general information on huge areas of interest. Most offer their help and advice for free. It's one of the beauties of the internet.

www.allexperts.com/index.htm			
All Experts			
Overall rating: ★★★★★			
Classification: Reference		**Content:**	★★★★
Updating: Frequently		**Readability:**	★★★★
Navigation: ★★★★★		**Speed:**	★★★★★
US			

Apparently this is the 'oldest and largest free Q and A service on the internet'. So, obviously this should be one of your first stops for your research needs. Basically you click one of the 36 categories, which include, amongst others, Cultures, Games, Movies, Style, Pets and Industry. Depending on your subject choice, you may have to make one or two more clicks to whittle down your area of interest. Once there, choose a nice friendly, generous-with-their-time volunteer experts and simply send them your question.

You will see that volunteers have a short description about who they are, what their area of expertise is and what sort of questions they are happy to answer. Make sure you ask the most appropriate expert. The experts for any particular topic can be arranged by a number of factors toward the bottom of the page. These include, Knowledge, Timeliness of Response, General Prestige, and Number of Questions Asked.

That is basically it. You send in a question, they answer it. Simple and free.

OTHER FEATURES

Our Service Find here why they do it, what their policies are and a little more in the way of background.

Newsletter On many of the pages you will see a small box inviting you to sign up for the free newsletter. All they require is your name and email address.

If you want a specific answer to a specific question you need an expert. All Experts has hundreds of them.

www.babynamer.com
Baby Namer

Overall rating: ★ ★ ★ ★			
Classification:	Reference	**Content:**	★ ★ ★ ★ ★
Updating:	Regularly	**Readability:**	★ ★ ★ ★ ★
Navigation:	★ ★ ★ ★ ★	**Speed:**	★ ★ ★ ★

(US)

Sometimes finding names for your characters can have you wasting lots and lots of valuable writing time. This site should be able to help out. It's set up to help soon-to-be parents pick names for their new arrivals, but the writer can utilise it just as well. More than 23,000 names are kept in their database, but this is more than simply a site that lists names. This site is obsessed with them. Type any name in the search box on the homepage and you'll see what we're on about. Most of the site's features are found once a name has been chosen. Another feature is the drop down box above the search facility on the homepage. Details of all this below. Remember, most data is from US census material, so is accurate over there, rather than over here. For a UK site, with only half the names and nowhere near as many features try www.namingbaby.co.uk.

For some reason, not all the following features are available for each name.

SPECIAL FEATURES

Select a List Available from the box above the search feature. Choose Popularity, Namesakes, Reviewers or Meaning and get names that fit the criteria.

Name Page This is where you start. Where you'll find out which countries use the name and some background to where it originates from. Then you can check names that are similar to this one. And why not click Try It Out to hear the name spoken out loud, in an American accent, naturally.

Namesakes The scourge of name choosing. So many names remind you of people who taint the image of the name. Choosing this from the drop-down list, rather than the name page, simply lists the names of famous or notable persons who share the name, including Leaders, personalities from Television and Film, and Literature. There are loads.

Perceptions Visitors to the site wax lyrical about their perceptions about the names.

Survey Your thoughts on names are required. You will be surprised at just how many people have given their views on whether a name gives an air of energy, warmth or intelligence.

Drawbacks A list of potential nicknames. Feel free to send in more of your own.

Other Features You can see the name of choice with the surname of choice, see the initials and see if they stand for anything unsavoury.

Both useful and fun crammed with information about names. Will make your head spin.

www.bartleby.com/index.html
Bartleby.com

Overall rating: ★★★★		
Classification: Reference	**Content:**	★★★★★
Updating: Daily	**Readability:**	★★★★★
Navigation: ★★★★★	**Speed:**	★★★★★

US

Free literature online. That would be the simple way of summing up Bartleby, but it doesn't go anywhere near to describing the wealth of information available. There are more than thirty reference texts, including thesauri, quotations, dictionaries, books on usage, mythology. There are a further seventeen collections of verse and almost thirty writers of verse can be accessed individually, from Virgil and Shakespeare to TS Elliot and Siegfried Sassoon. There's also a huge selection of titles in the Fiction section. Authors from Aristophanes to Agatha Christie have at least one of their works available for you to read online. Then there are lots of non-fiction, letters, papers and essays. You would need reinforced bookshelves at home to carry all these tomes. There are also daily and weekly features.

The site is extremely user friendly. The four sections above are navigated using the four drop-down boxes towards the top right of the home page or by clicking the four grey tabs in the title bar. Some of the most popular titles have independent links as well, running down the column beneath the drop down-boxes. Everything has links to further areas of interest, and if you can't find exactly what you want, try the search engine at the very top of every page.

SPECIAL FEATURES

Reference Some of the worlds most famous texts are here, in their entirety and for free. The World Fact Book. The Bible. The Oxford Shakespeare. Gray's Anatomy of the Human Body. Roget's Thesauri. The Elements of Style. And there's more. All the texts are very easy to browse. Simply choose from the options each new page presents until you get to exactly what you want.

Verse Absolutely free collection of verse from some of the world's greatest poets. Dozens of Anthologies and Volumes to read online.

Fiction Huge collection of whole texts of some of the world's most famous books. Great as a reference tool, or just to while away an evening or more, reading some classic fiction. For free, obviously.

Nonfiction With a slight leaning toward American works, this section is no less impressive than the rest of the site. Darwin's Origin of the Species sits quite comfortably alongside The Sayings of Confucius. Dozens of these titles are ones you meant to read but never got around to. Now you have no excuse.

Absolutely superb reference site. Can't fault it.

http://bubl.ac.uk/link/index.html
BUBL LINK

Overall rating: ★ ★ ★ ★ ★			
Classification: Portal		Content:	★ ★ ★ ★ ★
Updating: Monthly		Readability:	★ ★ ★ ★ ★
Navigation: ★ ★ ★ ★ ★		Speed:	★ ★ ★ ★ ★

UK

Simply astounding collection of links to all the academic subject areas you could possibly think of while still in your right mind. Although based in Scotland, this site has links to the whole world. The site is exceptionally simple to use. From the front page, either enter text in the search box, choose a letter of the alphabet or click that category that interests you. A few further clicks may be required to whittle down the links. When you get down to individual entries, it's amazing that each one has a short blurb, rather than simply just an address, like a lot of listings sites. This way you will spend less time wandering around sites that are not of specific use.

There are no features as such, just lots and lots of links to a ridiculous amount of information. There are 149 dictionaries, 109 links to biography related sites and 49 links to sites containing hundreds of mailing lists. We have barely scratched the service of what is contained in the General Reference section of the site, never mind the Creative Arts; Humanities; Language, Literature and Culture; Social Sciences; Engineering and Technology; Health Studies; Life Sciences; Mathematics and Computing; and Physical Sciences. No matter how small the piece of information you require, there is a very good chance that this site will lead you to it.

Whatever you're researching you will find help here, fear not.

www.copseek.com
CopSeek.com

Overall rating: ★ ★ ★ ★			
Classification: Portal		Content:	★ ★ ★ ★ ★
Updating: Daily		Readability:	★ ★ ★ ★
Navigation: ★ ★ ★ ★		Speed:	★ ★ ★ ★ ★

US

At some time in your writing career you will write about a Policeman. Whether you have a romantic heroine falling for the local copper, or a crack house raided by an armed response unit, you will want to make sure your portrayal is accurate. And unless you are a member of the Police, it may be very difficult to find out what you need to know. Until now. CopSeek is a portal site that lists nothing but Police related websites. It's an American site, so much of the content is about 'law enforcement Officers' rather than the 'Bobby on the beat', but there is still plenty for the writer looking for British related material.

The site is fussy looking, riddled with dozens of links. Particular areas of interest are categorised down the centre of the home page. Want more detailed headings? Try 'Click Here' for a complete listing of all the sites in alphabetical order. Use the search engine at the top of the home page for even more specific information. British writers might like to try searching for 'UK', then selecting 'Law Enforcement: United Kingdom' from the subsequent list, for a list of more geographically specific sites.

It is important to point out that this is not a site that has anything to do with writers. It's not geared to them and it doesn't offer to cater for them. This is a true blue, working Policeman site, and no one guarantees your research will be welcome or successful. But with all this expertise lying around, you have an excellent chance of finding out everything that you need.

SPECIAL FEATURES

Products Directory Located on the right of the homepage, this list links you to sites that deal with all manner of police related products. They include Knives, Body Armour, Firearms, Tactical-Duty Equipment and even Horse Products. Clicking any of these brings up a list of related sites. For example, clicking Firearms returned no fewer than 67 relevant sites. Any of these may be able to answer your questions about firearms and their usage.

Officer's Home Pages Close to five hundred officers have linked their personal homepages to this site. Most are in the USA but there are currently 13 UK links. Non of them are volunteering for this, but who knows, they might be willing to answer a question or two.

Other Features You can sign up for a free newsletter and be kept informed about new sites and relevant information. There's also a gift shop, a chat room, a book store, and even an auction room where most of the sections are disappointingly empty, but this section hasn't really got going yet.

As a starting place for world-wide Police research, you surely couldn't find better.

---

www.crime-scene-investigator.net
Crime Scene Investigator

Overall rating: ★★★★			
Classification:	Reference	Content:	★★★★★
Updating:	Regularly	Readability:	★★★★★
Navigation:	★★★★★	Speed:	★★★★★

(US)

We've seen crime scenes a hundred times in Hollywood films, but for a true picture of what happens and what the Police do, you can do no better than this site. It is incredibly detailed and yet easier to understand and follow than many other sites on the subject. Click the First Visit link that advises people how to make the most of the site, depending on your reason for being here. There's even advice specifically for writers, which can't be bad. The contents run down the centre of the page.

SPECIAL FEATURES

Crime Scene Response Here you'll find out what really goes on, who is involved, how the Police work and what they're looking for. There are a handful of fascinating articles too.

Evidence Collection Brilliantly simple list of how evidence should be collected. Lots of articles and further links make sure you won't make a mistake in your writing. Articles include the Dead Body Evidence Checklist and Protecting the Crime Scene. Other website links are offered for further research.

Crime Scene and Evidence Photography Loads more articles including the use of video, ultraviolet, infrared and digital photography. There is a useful list of further sites of interest from around the internet.

Other Features Lots of articles on fingerprints, general crime scene investigation, packaging evidence and even human remains. There are more links, a bookstore and details about training and employment for investigators.

Extremely detailed and informative site that provides all your crime scene research.

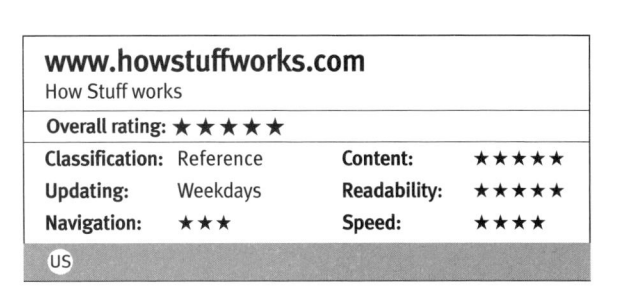

www.howstuffworks.com				
How Stuff works				
Overall rating: ★ ★ ★ ★ ★				
Classification:	Reference		**Content:**	★ ★ ★ ★ ★
Updating:	Weekdays		**Readability:**	★ ★ ★ ★ ★
Navigation:	★ ★ ★		**Speed:**	★ ★ ★ ★
US				

Like any child with an enquiring mind, or an adult armed with a screwdriver and a broken toaster, we all want to know how things work. When writing, it is essential that we get our facts right. As has been said elsewhere in this guide, writers who don't get their facts straight, or fail to research properly, get found out. However, information can also be a source of inspiration for plots, characters and twists and turns in any novel or screenplay. This site is a massive library of articles about how things work, from how air bags work to how second world war fighter planes worked. It's a busily designed site, with icons and links all over the place, catching your eye and threatening to keep you there for hours, becoming more and more fascinated. The features are not strictly 'features' as such, rather they are various sections which are detailed below. The links are all over the place, but browsing here is half the fun. You never know what you might find next.

SPECIAL FEATURES

Super Categories All the 'How do...?' Stuff organised into easier to manage sections.

Top Ten Articles / Questions The most popular stuff on the site.

Huge Question Archive Every article in an alphabetical list.

Cool Stuff Includes the fascinating section How Stuff WILL Work.

Masses of fascinating and thought provoking articles whether you're currently writing or not.

www.itools.com				
iTools				
Overall rating: ★★★★				
Classification:	Portal	**Content:**		★★★★★
Updating:	Occasionally	**Readability:**		★★★★★
Navigation:	★★★★★	**Speed:**		★★★★★
US				

As you may have noticed, there are lots and lots of sites offering access to information to help with your research. Many of them require you to do a lot of browsing after they have pointed you generally in right direction. The beauty of iTools is it's simplicity. You won't find anything wasted on flashy design, all the energies in this site have been channelled into getting you what you want as quickly as possible. The site still looks very professional and has a very reassuring air that convinces you that finding what you want will not be a problem. From the front page, three sets of tools are available. Insert the word, click the button, and you're away.

SPECIAL FEATURES

Language Tools The newest addition to the site and unbelievably easy to use. It is split into two sections, Look Up Words and Translate Language.

There are six dictionaries in which you can look for the word that's giving you trouble. Five dictionaries of technical terminology, a thesaurus, with specific sections for finding Rhymes, Synonyms and more. There's even a simple to use crossword solver and a scrabble tool.

In the Translate section a single word from 15 languages can be translated into any of the others. A very powerful tool. Finally there is a service that will translate an entire web page from one language to another. Simply insert the page address.

Research Tools A wealth of reference texts at your fingertips. The process for finding information is the same throughout the page. Find the title you want to use, type in the text and press the relevant button. Problem solved. Reference tools include Biographical Dictionary, Law Titles and even a trademark search.

Once again, each of these features takes you out of iTools to the site offering the service.

Search Tools Simple page that lets you search the Web, Newsgroups, and also to search for People or Business.

OTHER FEATURES

There's a currency converter, American maps and driving directions, as well as a whole range of internet tools.

Lots of essential reference tools all in one place.

www.publist.com
Pub List

Overall rating: ★★★★★		
Classification: Reference	**Content:**	★★★★
Updating: Regularly	**Readability:**	★★★★★
Navigation: ★★★★★	**Speed:**	★★★★

(US)

Don't expect to find listings for The Dog and Duck or The Rose and Crown, the Pubs referred to in the title of this site are Publications. There's quite a few of them too, at the last count, more than 150,000. Just take a moment to consider that in relation to world markets, titles to target your work at, reference potential, never mind creative encouragement. They come from all over the world, but the details are always given in English even if the actual magazine is not, so don't worry, at this stage, if you're not multi-lingual.

This is a simple site, both in design and use. It doesn't have any features as such, you simply type in the name of the publication you're interested in, or browse the titles by subject if your requirements are not quite so specific. A few more clicks will be required to whittle the huge database down to individual titles and their country of origin.

When you have chosen a single publication you are faced with a blue index card with four sections which list the following information.

Main The title's country of origin, frequency of publication, the publisher and some contact details. The publisher's name can be clicked for a full list of other titles they produce.

Publisher Provides further details of the company. Usually this includes the address, fax and telephone numbers.

Advertising For those wishing to buy space in the magazine. Interesting also to see the circulation figures which will give you a clearer picture of the type of magazine you're reading about.

Full Record All of the above in the same place at the same time.

Unbelievably comprehensive list of magazines and publications from all over the world.

www.refdesk.com			
Refdesk.com			
Overall rating: ★★★★★			
Classification:	Portal	Content:	★★★★★
Updating:	Daily	Readability:	★★★★
Navigation:	★★★★	Speed:	★★★★★
US			

Another very busy homepage that could give you a headache if you give in to it. The reason it's so busy? Well, it's quite simply huge. As far as facts go, it's like having the entire world at your fingertips. Navigation is both easy and yet a little complicated. If you're not sure where to start, it means lots of sifting through the little blue links. Adding a few more organised layers to the information, rather than throwing so much at you from the start might help simplify things. If you know exactly what you are looking for, type it into either the Google search engine, or the Search Refdesk box in the top left of the homepage. The first searches the whole internet, using, in our opinion, the best search engine there is. The second looks only in this site. For further surfing of the rest of the site, simply scroll down the homepage and find the yellow-headed section that best fits your requirements. Then click away until your thirst for knowledge is quenched.

SPECIAL FEATURES

Facts of the Day Daily Trivia, Picture of the Day, Moon Phases, Old Farmer's Almanac and more. Lots of interest. Lots here that will get you thinking about writing ideas and help to get the creativity flowing.

Facts-at-a-Glance Seemingly endless links to Dictionaries and Encyclopaedias on virtually every subject you can think about. Loads of 'Find' sites to help you research loads of topics including Legal, Medical and Military information. There's more information available here than you could possibly take in a lifetime.

Reference Resources A guide to their favourite pages, beginners guides to computer and internet usage, a homework helper, as well as a number of links to try and help you wade through the enormous amount of factual information available.

Just For Fun This is a surprisingly good section to help you come up with new ideas for both fiction and non-fiction projects. There are Useless Facts, Urban Legends, Greatest Films, Horoscopes and even Letterman Top Ten Lists.

Other Features A whole section dedicated to help and advice on how to 'do' things, including legal, financial and DIY links. The Subject Categories section is another way the site tries to point you in the right direction. Current News / Weather / Business / Sports keeps you up to date with news from around the world.

Amazing amount of links for facts and research.

www.rhymezone.com
RhymeZone.com

Overall rating: ★★★★★		
Classification: Reference	**Content:**	★★★★★
Updating: Occasionally	**Readability:**	★★★★★
Navigation: ★★★★★	**Speed:**	★★★★★

US

Extremely simple site but of great use to all poets, songwriters and even limerick writers. Non rhyming writers are not left out either, see below. Simply designed, it also loads quickly. The bulk of the site simply asks you to type in your current word of interest and then, using the drop-down box next to it, choose whether you want rhymes for that word, synonyms, antonyms, definitions, homophones (words that sound the same but are spelt differently) or even get lists of photographs containing the subject of your word. It's incredibly useful. The other excellent sections of interested are listed below. For all the entries below, the reader is invited to grade the quote, nursery rhyme, even the books of the Bible. The results are presented for all to see.

SPECIAL FEATURES

Shakespeare Search for quotations, by key word or even one word at a time. Pick the first word from a list of typical Shakespearean words. For example, Nay, Sir, Come, Marry, etc. Then you are offered some typical second words, until step by step you get the whole quotation. Interesting.

Quotations Search by last name or key word through hundreds of famous and not so famous quotes. From Douglas Adams and Edgar Allen Poe, to Frank Zappa Elizabeth Clarkson Zwart. The beauty of this collection of quotations is that it does not confine itself to classical writing and literature, or to stuffy old types waxing lyrical. As well as these you also get contemporary words by the likes of Miss Piggy, Alexi Sayle, and even Doctor Who.

Mother Goose Just about every children's nursery rhyme that you've ever heard of, and many more that will be new to you.

Famous Documents The bible at your fingertips. Chapter by chapter, the world's best selling book in its entirety. Also the U.S. Constitution and Declaration of Independence.

Other Features A logic game, some quizzes to test your vocabulary, and a feature for creating funny valentine couplets.

The rhyming feature alone makes this an extremely useful site. The additional features make it excellent.

www.firearmsid.com
FirearmsID.com

Overall rating: ★★★★		
Classification: Reference	**Content:**	★★★★
Updating: Occasionally	**Readability:**	★★★★★
Navigation: ★★★★	**Speed:**	★★★★

US

I may be a worrying sign of the times, but there is no getting away from it: more and more novels, stories and films contain guns. Almost always, they are pointed at people and fired. People get injured. People get killed. But when writing about it, it's not quite as simple as it sounds. If you don't have your facts straight about how the gun works and what results occur, someone, somewhere will spot it and delight in pointing out your poor research. But this site will go a long way to making sure your firearms information is accurate. Each month there is a featured article of interest. Most importantly you can find permanent information about what exactly happens when a weapon is fired. The links are all there on the homepage in four sections. Be prepared, not only is some of this quite heady in it's details, but the occasional page has unexpected groovy music.

SPECIAL FEATURES

Main Pages Details of safety devices on firearms; case profiles; the history of firearms identification. There are also detailed reports on how firearms, bullets and their casings are identified. Including even a fraction of the detail available will give enormous authenticity to your writing.

Misc Pages Featuring articles and illustrations of firearms, so you know what all the different components are called. There are some fascinating, but slow loading images of handguns and bullets. The Introduction to Ballistics is essential reading.

If you're writing about firearms, you need to know your stuff. You'll get a good grounding here.

www.askoxford.com
Ask Oxford

Overall rating: ★ ★ ★			
Classification:	Reference	**Content:**	★ ★ ★
Updating:	Daily	**Readability:**	★ ★ ★ ★ ★
Navigation:	★ ★ ★ ★ ★	**Speed:**	★ ★ ★ ★ ★

UK

This site is obsessed with the English language. From the homepage you will see articles about the nature of language and it's usage. At the time of writing they included articles about text messaging on mobile phones and quotations about Cricket. You will also find a Word of the Day, a Quote of the Week, a Quiz and a Crossword. However, as a reference tool you need to wander around the links at the top of the page. They're green and turn orange when your mouse pointer moves over them.

It never seems to go quite far enough though. All the sections are interesting as far as they do go. But lots of items seem a little like site padding.

SPECIAL FEATURES

Ask The Experts Want to know the collective name for a kind of animal? Herons? Snakes? Or maybe Baboons? Maybe you would rather check out some grammatical jargon. What exactly is the Superlative? Perhaps you would simply like to read the fascinating list of frequently asked questions about grammar, words and their origins, or spelling? Do it all here. And if you're still unsure about something, click the Oxford Word and Language Service link for further help.

World of Words Articles about language and its usage.

Better Writing Plain English, letter writing and a list of classic errors we make when writing.

Other Features A word game. A shop with a handful of writing usage titles. An interesting search facility that allows you to search the site, a dictionary and thesaurus, a book of first names.

Obsessed by language as far as it goes and hopefully will grow and grow.

OTHER SITES OF INTEREST

Encyclopaedia Britannica
http://www.britannica.com/

The mother of all reference works. You can search online through potted versions of the articles. If you want full access, you'll need to register. At $7.95 (US) a month it's not very expensive, but you can probably find equally detailed information by simply searching the internet. If you want to buy the 32 volume print version, the CD version, or the DVD version, as well as a number of related products point your browser at http://www.britannica.co.uk, where everything is priced in good old sterling but they prefer you to order something before telling you about delivery charges.

The Encyclopaedia Mythica
http://www.pantheon.org

Should you need to research Mythology, Folklore, Heroes or Beasts you should drop by this crisp, fast site. This is also a useful resource for finding ancient stories and folklore that can be adapted into more modern settings for your writing. Find great stories, mythical beasts and invaluable inspiration.

Forensic Science Resources
http://www.tncrimlaw.com/forensic/f_crimescene.html

A collection of links and a very detailed bibliography for all writers who need to know what goes on during crime scene investigation. From here you will be able to learn about clue finding, the use of photographs, scene reconstruction and a wealth of other forensic information. The bibliography also includes loads of links including the FBI homepage. This site is American, so if your story is based elsewhere, the information might not be quite as accurate.

Info Please
http://www.infoplease.com/

Another portal leading to more information than you could possibly take in during many lifetimes. The homepage is brimming with features and links, but the most efficient way to get around is to browse the almanacs in the lower half of the homepage. There are hundreds of articles under headings including Sports, World, Biography, Health and Science, Weather and Climate, and all the information is held here, so you won't suddenly find yourself at another site you've never seen before. Lots of scope for non-fiction and fiction writers alike.

Mystery Writer's Resources
http://www.zott.com/mysforum/links.htm

Part of the Mystery Writer's Forum, this is a comprehensive list of links for writers in the genre. There are links concerning Forensics, Law, Police Procedure, Guns, Poisons, Mafia and security. Add to this some more general links to Publishers, E-publishing and Agents, and Mystery Writers can feel suitably spoiled for choice.

The Phobia List
http://www.phobialist.com/

Comprehensive list of things people are afraid of, and their correct names. Great for giving interesting character traits of simply research purposes. Some of the fears seem to repeat occasionally with different names, but don't worry, there are hundreds of individual ones. They range from Ablutophobia, the fear of washing or bathing to Zemmiphobia, the fear of the great mole rat. All definitions claim to be researched rather than made up.

Xrefer
http://www.xrefer.com

More than 50 reference text collected together. It includes Dictionaries and Thesauri, Encyclopaedias, and quotations. The beauty of this site is that a single piece of text can be searched for in a number of resources at the same time without being dragged away to another site that holds the information. The results of your query are returned with a brief description, where the item is taken from and a link to the reference itself. Quick and reliable, and after a while even the annoying pop-up windows become insignificant in this simply excellent resource.

Chapter 08
screenwriting/playwriting

Simply having the ability to watch a film and think 'I could do better than that', is actually no indication that you can come up with the goods. If you want to write and sell scripts you have to know what you're doing. Sounds obvious? It should be, but most writers fail at the first hurdle because they haven't a clue. That's not to say they have no talent. Not at all. But a lack of experience can make a script look poor. So, to stop yourself writing half a dozen 'poor' scripts while you try to gain some 'experience', you might try soaking up as much scriptwriting information as you can. That is something the internet is not short on.

Screenwriting is one of the most popular writing genres represented on the web. This chapter does also include sites for theatre and TV writers, but the emphasis is with the hugely popular screenwriting sites. There are literally hundreds of pages offering help, advice, services, contacts and more. The following chapter includes the cream of the crop. Each one of them will make you a better screenwriter and help you to finish your script. The rewards may be glamorous, but huge effort, dedication and hard work are essential to any success. There's no easy route, but the journey is easier with the help of these sites than without.

www.craftyscreenwriting.com		
Crafty Screenwriting		
Overall rating: ★ ★ ★ ★		
Classification: Book	**Content:**	★ ★ ★ ★ ★
Updating: Fortnightly	**Readability:**	★ ★ ★ ★ ★
Navigation: ★ ★ ★ ★ ★	**Speed:**	★ ★ ★ ★ ★
(CAN)		

There are lots of books on screenwriting. Simply browsing the shelves in a single decent book shop can become quite daunting. So, how do you choose which books to buy, without spending hours standing in the shop reading and taking notes? Well, as great believers in 'something for nothing' we'd recommend going for those books that are free. Of which there are none. Which is why we worship the internet. This entire site is a free book. Written by a screenwriter/development executive who makes a living working on films that actually get made, (as opposed to those that gather dust in bottom drawers).. It's a simple site with little in the way of thrilling design, but this means it loads quickly which gets a large thumbs up from us. Another plus point is that the chapters are broken down into small manageable segments, so when you're after specifics, simply scroll down the longish list of contents from the front page and click on the relevant link, whether it's Basic Format or Never Make Your Characters Stupider Than You Are.

Just start with the excellent Beginning Screenwriting sections, then move onto the Intermediate Screenwriting stuff. It's all simple to follow and well worth the time spent taking it all in.

SPECIAL FEATURES

Frequently Asked Questions Aside from the book itself and some links, this is the only other section to mention. The links take you to a long, long page of FAQs, relating to both Screenwriting and the Motion Picture Industry. All good stuff. Get reading.

It's really good. It's free. Get in there and soak it all up.

www.createyourscreenplay.com
Create Your Screenplay

Overall rating: ★ ★ ★ ★		
Classification: Guide	Content:	★ ★ ★ ★ ★
Updating:	Readability:	★ ★ ★ ★ ★
Navigation: ★ ★ ★ ★ ★	Speed:	★ ★ ★ ★ ★

(CAN)

Barry Pearson is not a name that many in the UK will necessarily be familiar with, but he has been credited writer on eight feature films, has written more than 40 hours of television drama and produced 150 more. He also teaches a screenwriting seminar. Which is a pretty good track record. Some of the site is written in the style of a screenplay, so you can't really complain about the Courier type font used throughout, it's authentic. But it doesn't make for the easiest browsing.

From the first page click the Enter link to get to the site proper. While your at it make sure you sign up for the free Newsletter. Once inside, Barry has picked out the choice sections, and continuing the screenplay style, the links and descriptions read like short scene introductions from a film. The complete list of navigation links is at the bottom of this page. Each click opens up in a new page. Many of the features of Create Your Screenplay are accessed from links peppered throughout the site, many of which have different formatting altogether. Same information, different design. No explanation.

One of the appealing things about this site is that as well as giving you help, advice and tips from his own experience, Barry has also gone to the trouble of collecting essays and articles from all over the internet, written by dozens of industry professionals. He's arranged them in easy to browse categories, and then offered them to you as additional help. The beauty of this is that, in an industry where everyone talks about hard and fast 'rules' and then dozens of people do things differently, you can get an objective view. The more opinion you can soak up, the better.

SPECIAL FEATURES

Writing Help An excellent page discusses the scourge of all first time screenwriters: Formatting. It is guaranteed that you will read other formatting guides and they will vary slightly from this, but these are so detailed you could follow these guidelines to the letter and few would complain. You'll also find a couple of oddly formatted but wonderfully informative pages on screenplay structure and genres. The genre page is also a good tool for brainstorming ideas. Barry also gives you access to some excellent articles he penned himself and a brief FAQ section.

Index to Screenplay Writing Articles Quite simply a library of articles from around the net. From Structure and Character to Pitching and Selling. Virtually everything you can think of is here. All the links take you to the sites that hold the articles.

Research Huge list of links for all manner of research.

Other Features There is a wealth of information about the next screenwriting seminar, but unless you're in, or planning a jaunt to, Canada, it's going to be a little difficult to take part. Just in case you think there's not enough for you here, the Links page is bursting with other screenwriting related sites. There is also a Screenplay Development Service, which produces a very detailed report on your script. Like all these services it is quite expensive, but you only pay the second half of the fee when your screenplay is sold.

You will immediately feel in safe hands at this simply superb site.

www.scriptsales.com
Done Deal

Overall rating: ★★★★★			
Classification:	Guide	Content:	★★★★★
Updating:	Daily	Readability:	★★★★★
Navigation:	★★★★★	Speed:	★★★★★

(US)

There will come a time, especially if you use the excellent advice of the sites in this chapter, when you have a decent, properly constructed and formatted screenplay finished. You can't improve it. So what to do next? Sell it. Seems like a good idea. Why not, people sell scripts every day?

This site is a guide to the post-writing process when you see your work bought and then made into a film. Simple? Not really, no. However, this site can keep you up to date with what's going on in the world of film script sales. It also tells you where you can look for representation in America, which is, obviously, where most of the script deals are done.

Navigate using the blue section down the left, or virtually the same links in the body of the home page.

SPECIAL FEATURES

Agency & Managers Dozens of names, address and contact numbers for Agents and Managers based in New York and Los Angeles. These are the people who can help you sell your film.

Sales Archives Click on a month and prepare to be astounded at how many scripts have been sold, and of course, this is not every single sale, some will no doubt have been missed. All these positive dealing should encourage you. People really do sell scripts. This just might give you the tiny glimmer of optimism for your own script.

Examples As if writing the script wasn't hard enough, you still need to fathom query letters, option agreements, release forms, treatments and step outlines. Here you'll find examples of all these and the other nitty-gritty bits and pieces you'll encounter on the road to a deal.

Production Companies These people make films and might want to see your script. They might not. But at least you now know where they are and how to contact them.

Hollywhooped Another expert answers more questions. They're friendly, sensible and authoritative replies to pressing issues. If you've been looking at a lot of screenwriting sites, you'll have seen that the same questions keep coming up again and again, and all the answers are basically the same. Soon you'll have nothing left to ask and will be able to get on with the hard bit – writing.

OTHER FEATURES

Fundamentals Check your story and characters are up to scratch and check that you understand all the film making jargon in the Glossary.

Interviews The more you can get inside the heads of working professionals, the better chance you have of following in their footsteps. All these guys make money writing. They must know what they're doing. Read them all.

Read Again, there's lots of advice out there, most of it saying the same things. Read it, learn it, act on it.

Community Message board, chat room and cork board for small ads. This is also where you can sign up for the free monthly newsletter.

Other Features Unusually, part of this site is included again in this Good Web Guide. Check out their other entry in the For Sale chapter.

It's great to know that there's help for you once your script is finished. Excellent content.

www.script-o-rama.com
Drew's Script-O-Rama

Overall rating: ★ ★ ★ ★ ★			
Classification:	Homepage	**Content:**	★ ★ ★ ★ ★
Updating:	Regularly	**Readability:**	★ ★ ★ ★ ★
Navigation:	★ ★ ★ ★	**Speed:**	★ ★ ★ ★ ★

(US)

It's long been said that you can't 'write' unless you 'read'. Reading professionally produced or published work is one of the best ways of learning your craft. With screenplays it's a little harder to find scripts than it is for, say, a novelist to find novels. Even harder to find them for free. But never fear, once again the internet delivers exactly what you need. Drew has a huge collection of scripts that you can download for absolutely nothing. You can see how the words on the original pages became the films you enjoyed on the big screen. From the front page you have to choose whether you want the Snazzy or Normal version of the site. Same site, different design. We choose snazzy every time. Then simply move your mouse around the picture to discover which bits take you where. This is slightly irritating, but you'll get over it. The screenplays are found by clicking the bottom left hand corner of the smoky club picture. The site loads pretty quickly, while the scripts' download times vary depending on how long the film script is and what format it has been saved in. You want to write scripts? Then you have to read some. As many as you can. There's no way round it.

SPECIAL FEATURES

Scripts and Transcripts You can download film scripts. Interestingly, you don't always just get the one script for the one film. There are a variety of drafts. From barely recognisable first drafts to the much more familiar final shooting scripts. Interesting to see how a film develops from early drafts to the finished article. But that's not all. How about TV scripts, transcripts and even scripts yet to made, possibly written by people just like you. Choose the different parts of the alphabet from the top and the scripts, beginning with those letters can be, scrolled through underneath.

OTHER FEATURES

You'll also find an interesting, but short, sections on some scenes that didn't make it into the finished film, Links, Polls, and even Haiku poetry, which for some unknown reason seems to becoming more and more popular on all sorts of web sites. Read it and go 'huh?'

Surely the biggest collection of free film scripts outside of Hollywood. Read 'em if you want to write 'em.

www.moviebytes.com
Movie Bytes

Overall rating: ★★★★★		
Classification:	CompetitionPortal	
Updating:	Daily	
Navigation: ★★★★★		
Content:		★★★★★
Readability:		★★★★★
Speed:		★★★★★

US

Oh so many screenwriting contests. Having a deadline for a contest is a great way of motivating yourself to finish your screenplay. However, there are so many here, that if you miss your initial deadline, there's always another one, for a different competition, just around the corner. Perhaps you'll have to rely on self motivation after all.

The homepage to this information stacked site is sensibly laid out. The links are easy to access, at the top of the page, in the blue stripe. Down the centre of the page are the latest bits of news, then the new contest announcements, then the all important information on the contests you're going to miss if you don't get a move on. Then, almost at the bottom are the site sponsors. A tiny scroll further and you'll find the form to fill in if you want the free newsletter and access to more of the site via a password they'll send you. You want this, so fill it in. Good luck with the competitions.

SPECIAL FEATURES

Contests It's why you're here. If you like long lists, and you have nothing better to do for the rest of the day, you can see all the contests together, alphabetically. At the time of writing their were a mere 209 for you to browse. A much better idea is to look at the subsections running down this page and see which one is closest to your needs. Some contests are parts of festivals, others encourage minority entries, some are for short screenplays, while others are interested in scripts for TV. Some of them are available to enter for free. Each contest has a brief blurb detailing what it's all about and the all important deadline. If you click the title of a contest you go to a full page with more detailed information. Make sure to check whether a contest is accepting entries from your part of the world before sending an entry.

Writers Wanted Lots of production companies asking for scripts. Nearly all of them American, but that needn't be a problem.

Bulletin Board As soon as you subscribe to the newsletter you will be sent a password which you need to access this section. Once in you see that this a fairly active board, without being overwhelming. Threads with most recent responses are at the top. There is a great deal of intelligent comment going on here. It will also help to remind you, that as a screenwriter, you are not alone.

Other Features A huge list of names and addresses of US based writer's agents. Also, news stories, going as far back as a year ago, about competitions.

Professional site, great content, intelligent bulletin board. Bookmark it and come back often.

www.vcu.edu/artweb/playwriting
The Playwriting Seminars

Overall rating: ★★★★★		
Classification: Guide	Content:	★★★★★
Updating: Two monthly	Readability:	★★★★★
Navigation: ★★★★★	Speed:	★★★★★

US

A 230 page guide to the art and craft of writing stage plays. This relaxed yet detailed site takes you step by step through the process of scriptwriting for the theatre. Peppered throughout with quotes from professionals, the guide has a friendly tone that doesn't bog you down with pages of technical detail and academic-sounding user-unfriendly text. It's concise and it's an enjoyable read. To get going, click the title of the page. Once inside you can begin with Primary Areas of The Playwriting Seminars and work through them, step by step. Or if you prefer, you can make straight for the area that interests you most and use the manual as more of a 'dip in' guide. Whichever you choose, once you are reading through, each page offers you further links to recommended next sections, so there is no need to even used the Back button.

SPECIAL FEATURES

Content The mechanics of your plot are covered in detail. From Characters and Setting to Themes and Voice. No matter what you are writing about, these are the building blocks by which your script will succeed or fail.

Film No matter how 'pure' your love of writing for the stage, it is almost certain that at some point you will toy with the idea of writing for the screen. The differences between the disciplines are discussed, as are the realities of what to expect if you take on a screenplay. Basic tips and page layout are both covered, there are even a few suggestions of what to do with the script when it's finished.

Structure How many characters? How long should the play run? How about shape and style and getting the audience to come along with you willingly? Tricks of the trade to make your script work.

Working It's all very well having a good idea and knowing something about how to structure a plot and write believable characters. What about actually getting that story and that knowledge down on paper? Should you work from an outline? What about revisions? And what about the terrible times when the block descends and you can't come up with a single new word or idea? All is explained.

Format It may not be at the top of your list of important things right now, but when you have finished the script, if it is not set out in the right way it will stand out as an amateurish piece of work. Learn how to do it the professional way.

Business If you want to be taken seriously and you want to make a business out of your scriptwriting, you'll need to know a little about how the business works. Keep in mind that the information in this section is heavily biased towards American writers and the information may not apply in quite the same way, elsewhere in the world.

A wonderful, easygoing site, crammed with essential information for playwrights.

www.screenwriterscyberia.com
Screenwriters Cyberia

Overall rating: ★★★★		
Classification: Portal	**Content:**	★★★★★
Updating: Fortnightly	**Readability:**	★★★★
Navigation: ★★★★	**Speed:**	★★★

(US)

The New Stuff scrolls across the top of the home page. Click What's New to see the latest site additions. Down the left of the page are a list of some of the most pressing concerns to anyone writing screenplays, from Agents and Film Schools to Coverage and Competitions. Click any of them and suddenly you are faced with more sites, more useful stuff, more help and advice than you thought possible. There's even a Play Room for when the writing world all gets too much for you.

The site design is not where the time and energy have been spent on this site, but who cares, it's a wonderful resource and it loads quickly too.

SPECIAL FEATURES

Agents Online directories with lists of Agents, No-Fee Literary Agents and even Bad Agents to avoid. Continue down the page for more links to individual Agencies and Management and even addresses of the stars,

Production Companies Keen to cut out the middle man and approach the film makers straight away? Here they are.

Coverage These sites will look at your work, write a constructive report on it and, naturally, charge you for the service. Classes and seminars are included here too.

Studios These are the big guns of American TV and film entertainment. The BBC also get a link, along with more than 50 others.

Software You no doubt have come across the biggest software titles for helping writers, but on this page you will find many more. Some are web based, some have downloadable demo versions and some are absolutely free.

FAQs Not for this site, but rather a very useful page where links to Screenwriting frequently asked questions from other sites are listed. There's a wealth of information as well as details of newsgroups and newsletters.

The Play Room Fancy a small diversion from writing. There are hours worth of distractions, all film related, and many of them quite amusing.

Other Features If you want sites dedicated to finished films, and the business of Hollywood, click The Biz. The section In Print has lots of magazines, books and reference titles that all exist in the real world rather than in cyber space. Click Competitions for basic details and links for loads of prize winning possibilities. There's a comprehensive list of Film Festivals, places to obtain screenplays, and a page listing screenwriter's own web sites.

As screenwriting portal sites go, this is excellent and certainly one you should visit.

www.screenwritersutopia.com
The Screenwriters Utopia

Overall rating: ★★★★			
Classification:	Portal	Content:	★★★★★
Updating:	Daily	Readability:	★★★★
Navigation:	★★★★	Speed:	★★★★★

US

Let me start by saying '3000 pages of web content', then add to that '100,000 monthly visitors', and end by mentioning that Chris Wehner, who runs the site, is a screenwriter, web editor and also writes regular columns covering 'Hollywood and screenwriting'. That should be more than enough encouragement for you to fire up your browsers and get online.

Firstly, and it's the only criticism we have, the home page is daunting. The lists of links are formidable, and could maybe put you off on a first visit. But stick with it and the mist starts to clear. Down the right of centre, the blue links are simply news. Every time you arrive at the site, check here to see what's going on in the industry. The left of centre is where the features live, more of those below. The extreme left is a sort of site guide, the best bits you will also find below.

SPECIAL FEATURES

Today's News Fairly self-explanatory. However, you won't find traditional film info as such. This is totally about the writers. You'll read who has just been attached to which project and all the insider news regarding scripts in the pipeline. It's fascinating to realise that some of these are the films that will be box office smashes in the future, but at the moment you're one of a small group who have even heard of them. Under the main heading for News is the link Script Sales, where you can read short items on who has sold what to whom.

Features One of the beauties (and ironically, also one of the frustrations) of this section is that there is no guide how to work through the information available to make you a better writer and help you sell your work. So, you wander the columns and click on titles that take your fancy. Then you realise it's all good stuff. Really good stuff, and you think you may have to phone work and feign illness in order to take it all in. The articles all manage to have a conversational tone that so many books on screenwriting fail to achieve. You actually enjoy reading the articles and gain masses of invaluable knowledge, without really having to try. This is our kind of learning. That's not to say your successful screenplay will be any easier to write, but at least you'll feel you know a little more about what you're trying to do.

Script Reviews You won't realise how incredibly useful this is until you've read a few. These are not reviews of the films, but reviews of the cold, black type on crisp white paper, scripts. It's a superb insight into how an intelligent reader can slate or extol the virtues of your work. Beware, the reviews contain spoilers which may upset your viewing pleasure when the films come out. If the Butler did it, it probably says so.

Work Shop Superb. Step by step guide to help you complete that screenplay. Articles, Q and A, and more.

Hollywood Internet Links to everything to do with Hollywood on the internet.

OTHER FEATURES

There are also polls, a contest guide and an ezine, which comes to you free every month.

The site gives you hope, encouragement and purpose. So much good stuff here you'll have to careful you don't forget to actually write you screenplay.

www.scriptshop.co.uk
Script Shop

Overall rating: ★★★★			
Classification:	Script promotion	**Content:**	★★★★★
Updating:	Frequently	**Readability:**	★★★★★
Navigation:	★★★★★	**Speed:**	★★★★★
UK			

As soon as you enter the above web address, the site appears, but the address turns into one of those horrible numbers addresses that are impossible to remember. We don't know why, but stick with the above address and ignore the numbers.

This is a very interesting UK site for screenwriters looking to find exposure for their finished scripts. Basically what happens is this: you send in your script, they decide if it's any good, if it is, it will be listed on the site and producers and companies will be encouraged to keep coming back to the site searching for talent. There's a fee for the process, which currently stands at £75 for reading and appraisal, and if it's selected for display on the site it'll cost you a further £75 for a period of four months. One of the huge pluses of this site is that they limit the content. This isn't a huge free for all where anyone can have everything they've ever written on display. They like to limit the site to 50 projects, each one has a brief synopsis, an equally brief readers review and rating out of ten for the main features of your script. If your work is rejected, your money is not wasted as you receive a professional reader's report on your script. You may choose to apply this advice to your script, and then resubmit it for a reduced fee.

In it's first twelve months the site had 10,000 hits, was asked by 26 companies to see full scripts and has seen one film made into a feature.

The site is attractive and very professional both in tone and design. The links are right there on the homepage, where you can't miss them.

SPECIAL FEATURES

About Scriptshop Learn what they are about and what they can do for you.

Guide For Writers Everything you need to know when submitting work. It includes prices, worries writers have about their ideas being stolen from the site, the all important address and more details of why you need this service.

View Scripts Anyone can view this section. Includes log lines and brief summaries of the scripts on offer.

Script Submission Fill out the form to send with your completed script.

Reader's CVs Very impressive list of professional who will be looking at the submitted scripts. You know you are in good hands. These guys know what they are talking about.

Newsboard see the success stories about scripts that the site has featured.

Great service. Hopefully it will help get your script seen by the people who matter.

http://scriptwritingsuccess.com/
Scriptwriting Success / The Scriptwriter's Niche

Overall rating: ★ ★ ★ ★			
Classification:	Guide	**Content:**	★ ★ ★ ★ ★
Updating:	Weekly	**Readability:**	★ ★ ★ ★ ★
Navigation:	★ ★ ★ ★ ★	**Speed:**	★ ★ ★ ★ ★

(UK)

Firstly, let me say, without reservation, this is a wonderful site. If you want to write screenplays then you cannot fail to become a better writer by soaking up the fountain of knowledge available here. However, it comes at a price. Currently it's $19.95 to get the whole site in electronic book format. Now, before you start frothing at the mouth with indignation for having to actually pay for something on the net, let me explain a few things. You're probably thinking you can find all this for nothing somewhere else on the internet. Possibly, but having it all in one place, all so well written, so friendly and with new content added every week will be hard to find. You certainly won't get the free bonus items offered here.

To ease your fevered mind regarding payments over the net, you pay via a secure server. There are also a variety of offers if you apply by a certain time. Add to this a whole year's guarantee, if you don't like what you've paid for (but you will) your money will be refunded. It all seems like a rather good deal to us. If you Click Here To Order Now you'll need to search for Scriptwriter's Niche, as it doesn't actually appear on the page that's selling it!

If you decide not to part with some cash, you can get no further than this homepage and its long, tempting, in-depth description of what you're missing.

But what do you get for you money? See below...

SPECIAL FEATURES

Scriptwriting Success A whole book. It's in Adobe PDF format, so you'll need the Acrobat Reader, which can be downloaded for free. Normally selling for twice the price of your monthly membership, this guide takes you every step of the way to a polished screenplay. It can't guarantee you millions or Oscars, but you'll have a much better idea of what's required for a successful screenplay. You'll learn how to get ideas, how to write a log line and a treatment and how to plan, write, polish and then sell your work. Then there are samples and case studies to give you a feel of what's required.

Film Scriptwriter's Jargon Buster Do you know your Slugline from your Logline? Your Dramatic Bump from a Set Piece? 60 terms that will never be a problem to you again.

The Screenplay Development Kit These are examples of all the different steps you will undertake on the way to completing your screenplay. From Log Line and Outline to First Draft and Final Polish. Every step of the way, these really helpful templates keep you on track.

Write On Time A short guide that will help you organise your time, find more time and use that time to write successfully. Now you've got no excuse not to get on with it.

Sell Your Script Speaks for itself, and gives some great pointers to your first sale.

Friendly, informative and user-friendly. Will gently turn you into a better screenwriter.

www.sydfield.com
SydField.com

Overall rating: ★★★★★			
Classification:	Official Site	**Content:**	★★★★★
Updating:	Occasionally	**Readability:**	★★★★★
Navigation:	★★★★★	**Speed:**	★★★★★

US

As voices in the world of screenwriting go, there are few that speak more prominently, or hold more respect then Mr. Syd Field. His fellow industry professionals admire and recommend him, his books are always in the lists of suggested reading on virtually every screenwriting site on the net. He's the boss. Ignore him at your peril. The downside to this colossus of American film writing is that, because he is so revered, his help, insight, thoughts and advice are, on the whole, not offered free gratis. But then again why should they be? His books are available to buy, there are online courses to enrol on, evaluations of your work can be ordered. But don't despair if money is tight, , like most experts on the internet he doesn't mind sharing some of his knowledge for free. Details below.

The various coloured parts of the homepage can be clicked for a variety of information, but we recommend clicking the Enter link on the blue page. You won't miss out on anything as all these links are available as links on the left of every page, under the yellow pen nib icon. You'll soon realise that this site has had quite some time and effort spent on it's design and that there is very little waiting around for pages to load into your browser. Very professional in every aspect of design.

SPECIAL FEATURES

About Syd Field Prepare to be impressed. Syd Field seems to have worked with everyone. He's been a consultant for some of the world's biggest film companies, and he's even creative consultant to the Governments of Argentina, Austria, Brazil, and Mexico. And he looks a little like Art Garfunkel, which is neither here nor there.

Screenwriter's Corner Clicking this section takes you to a whole new site within the site. It's described as being an 'experiment', but it's really a community for screenwriters around the world. Within this section the links are on the left, as in the main site and include a Film of the Month where a classic film is examined for your benefit; a Q&A with Syd Field where he answers screenwriting questions; and some related links. It's also in this section where you can find out about online courses and pay for them securely online. There's another section where you can get free email, chat rooms and message boards.

Books and Videos No prizes for what's on offer here. His books can be clicked and you'll find yourself in the Syd Field section of The Writer's Store, where loads more, as well as the title you clicked, can be found and ordered. As always, if you're in the UK, look for these books in UK online stores like Amazon.co.uk., rather than ordering them all the way from America. A selection of videos are recommended for you to buy and study, they all link to the American version of Amazon.com.

Interviews with Writers Shame there are only four interviews so far. They make fascinating reading, especially as they have been carried out and guided by Syd Field, who obviously has your screenwriting education at heart. Reading these interviews also lets you understand why the videos in the above section were recommended. Read the interview then watch the film to get the very best out of the advice on offer.

Individual Consultations Odd that there is very little detail here about what you get and how much it costs, beyond the fact that it'll cost you $125 for fifteen minutes.

Calendar of Events Find out what's going on in the professional world of Syd Field, on a month by month basis.

If you want to learn about screenwriting, and have the money to spend, you may as well learn from the best. In many eyes, this is he.

www.xerif.com/index.html		
Virtual Script Workshop		
Overall rating: ★ ★ ★ ★		
Classification: Courses	**Content:**	★★★★★
Updating: Monthly	**Readability:**	★★★★
Navigation: ★★★★★	**Speed:**	★★★★★
(UK)		

Sometimes the wealth of articles, information and how-to sites might not be quite what you're looking for. Maybe you want to be given more personal help and assistance. Maybe you want a recognised qualification and certificate at the end of your study? Maybe you simply want to be able to get the above help from someone here in Britain. If so, you've come to the right place. This is a very simple site. Apart from the homepage, there are only four navigational links to other sections of the site. They are all available from the light green band running underneath the site header. However, this doesn't mean that the site is lacking by any means. What you're presented with is more than enough for you to find an excellent screenwriting course. And they are all available to undertake from the comfort of your own home.

SPECIAL FEATURES

Birkbeck Here you'll find news of the forthcoming courses from Birkbeck College, University of London. At the time of writing there was both a beginners and advanced course, both running for a ten week period. Follow the links to the Birkbeck homepage for further details.

VSW Directory Select your continent from the map of the world for a relevant list of sites that have offered online screenwriting courses in the last twelve months. Follow the links to those sites to see what's on offer today.

VSW Newsletter Keep up to date with news of new courses and activities. Sign up and have it sent straight to your email box.

Scriptunities Free monthly guide to competitions and opportunities for scriptwriters. Sign up by simply entering your email address. The latest issue can be downloaded as a PDF file. If you'd rather just see it as a web page, click the latest month's link and you'll be taken straight there. Don't be surprised to find a constant stream of exciting information, lots of details and links and useful things for you to keep an eye on in the coming months.

Excellent resource for easily finding an, online course in the UK.

---

www.wordplayer.com
Wordplay

Overall rating: ★★★★		
Classification: Guide	**Content:**	★★★★★
Updating: Occasionally	**Readability:**	★★★★★
Navigation: ★★★★★	**Speed:**	★★★★★

US

This is our favourite screenwriting site on the internet. Why? Because it's great. Why is it great? Because you know you've stumbled across something really special as a screenwriter. It's not the sort of site that visually grabs you. But don't give that a second thought. From the first few sentences you can see that the guys who run this site have a sense of humour, which helps when you're banging your head against the wall trying to get a script finished. Also, these guys, Ted Elliott and Terry Rossio are seasoned professionals. Their credits include The Mask of Zorro, Disney's animated feature Aladdin, Shrek, Antz, as well as the truly dreadful Godzilla, which they are happy to explain turned out to be very different from their original script. They hated the film too.

Everything on this site has a laid back feel to it. Ted and Terry have their feet up on the sofa while they wow you with just about everything you need to know, and every problem you've ever encountered whilst thrashing out a screenplay.

These guys are busy professionals, so the site is updated fairly irregularly, but there's plenty to get your teeth into while waiting for the next update. The six circles at the bottom of every page take you swiftly to your area of interest.

SPECIAL FEATURES

Columns This is more wisdom, straight from the horses mouth, than you could hope to find anywhere on the net.

You won't want to browse this section, you will want to start at the top and methodically take in every word. At the time of writing there were more than 40 columns. They not only advise on every aspect of the scriptwriting process, but also cover the business and what you might expect to encounter if you're ever out there playing with the Hollywood big boys.

Letters Fairly obvious to guess what goes on here. Answers to questions writers like you have sent in. But there is so much honesty here it's extremely refreshing, 'movies are fun, writing is hard'. It's nice to know they think so too.

Indy Pros Excellent interviews and discussions with some big names in the film world. Even if some of the names are unfamiliar you'll know their work, which includes Awakenings, Beverly Hills Cop and The Fly.

Archives Here, for your convenience you can download the Columns as text files or even have them sent to you via email. Three of their screenplays are available too.

So you know what to expect when your time comes, you can also see what a contract looks like. There are a host of other downloadable bits and pieces including Aristotle's Poetics and the fascinating 'Thirty-six Dramatic Situations', which explains every variation on a plot line that it is possible to conceive of.

Worth every second you spend here and worth missing the odd mildly important event in your own life, just to get to the end.

---

www.writernet.co.uk
Writernet

Overall rating: ★★★★

Classification:	Resource	**Content:**	★★★★★
Updating:	Frequently	**Readability:**	★★★★★
Navigation:	★★★★★	**Speed:**	★★★★★

UK

If you are a writer involved with the live or recorded industry, or if you want to write for any of the performance mediums, this site has been created to offer you a range of services that hope to further your career. Writers and Producers both use the site as a means of finding each other and working together. Click the About Us link for their mission statement and some sparkling recommendations from writers and producers. Then have a quick look at the Partners link to see that they have links with some fairly high profile groups.

It's very easy to get around and a pleasant cool blue design is appealing to the eye. The site links are always available in the column on the left.

To take full advantage of the services on offer, you need to register, which starts at a very reasonable £25 per year for an unwaged or student writer and £35 for a part waged writer. Presently, it is not possible to join up on line. Instead, there is a form which can printed and sent by traditional means.

SPECIAL FEATURES

Services Decide whether you are a Writer or a Producer and click the appropriate link. Then you try and remember whether you've subscribed or not. However, even if you haven't you can still get limited access to a number of sections. You will be told in quite some detail what information you are missing out on by not being a member. There's information about agents, courses theatre companies, awards and radio drama. Certainly whets the appetite. There is an exceptionally good value script reading service, that costs you even less as a paid up member. If you have a professional writing credit to your name you can add your name to the writer's database which will then be aimed at all the kinds of people who employ writers. And this service is free.

News A range of items about the site; the industry; and funding for writers.

Opportunities Fairly active list of job and training opportunities, but you can't get the full details without signing up and becoming a member.

Bulletin Board Industry events and large list of useful sites. These sections are available to everyone.

Publications Very reasonably priced, or even free, here are guides and reports offering advice on a range of writer related issues. There are also a mass of articles, each of which can be sent to you by post or email and costs a pound.

Links Theatre Companies, Funding Bodies, Organisations, TV Producers and more. Links lead offsite to the various homepages.

Excellent resource for professional UK writers.

www.wga.org/mentors/mentors.html			
Writers Guild of America Mentors			
Overall rating: ★ ★ ★ ★			
Classification:	Official site	Content:	★ ★ ★ ★ ★
Updating:	Occasionally	Readability:	★ ★ ★ ★ ★
Navigation:	★ ★ ★ ★ ★	Speed:	★ ★ ★ ★ ★
US			

You'll see from this guide that writers are a nice helpful bunch. They don't mind sharing their knowledge and helping you improve your writing by setting up many of the sites you'll find in this guide. Many of them, as you will have noticed, share their expertise simply out of the goodness of their hearts, not charging you a single penny. However, the Writers Guild of America has gone a small step further. They have collected together industry professionals who don't simply upload their knowledge onto web pages. These experts will directly answer any questions you put to them, concerning screenwriting, obviously. You simply scroll down the list and find a writer who is qualified in the areas that interest you, for example: feature films, independent films, comedy, documentary, animation or daytime serials. Then you email them your question. That's all there is to it. No courses to join or hefty fees to part with.

Don't be put off that none of the mentors have credits or even their full name on display, because, anonymous or not, they all know what they're talking about.

Because they're a busy lot, with projects of their own and mouths to fee, it's important to check out the three sections of Top Responses before you email a question, to see if it has already been covered. Don't be surprised if it has, these guys are pretty thorough. Once again, if only to underline the fact there is no charge, and no registration is required for this service.

No features, just a very useful, generous resource.

www.bbc.co.uk/writersroom
BBC – The Writers' Room

Overall rating: ★ ★ ★ ★			
Classification:	Guide	**Content:**	★ ★ ★ ★
Updating:	Monthly	**Readability:**	★ ★ ★ ★ ★
Navigation:	★ ★ ★ ★ ★	**Speed:**	★ ★ ★ ★ ★

(UK)

The BBC have made great TV programmes in the past, and not unsurprisingly, they're quite keen to make more. Which is where maybe you come in. The BBC are trying to make it easier for writers to submit their work, and have it accepted. Which is exactly what you want to hear. This site tells you what they're up to, new writing-wise. Just as importantly it helps you to avoid falling at the first hurdle with your writing submissions. To flesh the site out there are a couple of interviews with successful writers, but the Writers Guidelines are the invaluable part of the site.

Navigate using the white underlined links on the left or the rather more eye-catching links in the main body of the homepage. It's a nice looking site and loads quickly into your browser with very little hanging around.

SPECIAL FEATURES

Guidelines This section claims to be updated regularly and should be an immediate stopping place for writers wanting to submit comedy or drama for the TV or Radio. They are fairly brief details but tell you everything you need to know. Although the site is run by the BBC, obviously all the information is pretty relevant whoever you send your script to. You'll find out what the BBC are looking for, how to format it, who to send it to, and pitfalls to avoid. If your script complies with all this information, you'll have a much better chance of seeing a positive response.

Write Now Find out about the New Writing Initiative which is dedicated to finding, not surprisingly, new writers. They read unsolicited scripts and try to get to readings and screenings of your work. You and your work will be assessed for suitability with the BBC.

Message Board There are several here for you to participate in after you've registered (it's free). The two connected with the Writers' Room are the main ones of interest. Some fairly involved message discussions take place here on Comedy or Drama. Well worth a look and a good place to ask any further questions you might have.

OTHER FEATURES

Insight At the time of writing there was an interesting video interview with Lee Hall who penned Billy Elliot, where he talks about his views and experiences as a writer. You can download the necessary RealPlayer, if you don't have it.

Q and A Successful writers answer writing questions.

Loads of advice to help you submit and, hopefully, further your writing career.

www.madscreenwriter.com/navigate.htm
Mad Screenwriter

Overall rating: ★★★★		
Classification: Portal	Content:	★★★★
Updating: Monthly	Readability:	★★★★★
Navigation: ★★★★★	Speed:	★★★★★
CAN		

This site has lots. It's not only interested in writing, but the whole film making process too and even actors and artists get a look in. It's a simple, trendy, uncluttered looking site that simply shares the links that the nice people behind the site use. So, basically, it's a real dip-into site featuring loads of links, resources, bits of fun and trivia (the quotes pages should raise a smile, and make you wish you'd said it first). You'll notice that quite a few of the links appear in different sections of the site. Don't let this bother you, it's just their way of making sure you don't miss anything. And, anyway, it's quick, which scores loads of brownie points with us. The different sections are all there on the homepage. Enjoy.

SPECIAL FEATURES

Screen Writing Your first stop. Find advice, masses of resources, genre stuff, news, discussion groups, reference materials and even a whole section dedicated to the needs of Women writers which are generally sites by women and for women. However, guys, feel free to check these sites out too. As far as I remember, the last time I looked, good writing advice was pretty much universal.

There are loads more links to loads more writing related stuff. Not as thoroughly excellent as this Good Web Guide, obviously, but pretty good all the same.

DV Cafe Many writers, frustrated that they can't sell their superb film scripts, decide that the way to get noticed is to do it themselves. Produce their films and prove to the world that they were wrong to be overlooked. DV is the cheap, quick, trendy way to make films. If it's a foreign language to you, but seems like a good idea in principle, work your way through these links for help, advice and communities willing to give you moral support in your venture. This links are actually kept at another site, but don't hold that against them.

Television If this is the field you want to write for, then immerse yourself in plenty of industry information and keep up with the goings on by clicking your way through these links.

Search There is so much for you to work through here, that frustrations might set in if you are not finding the desired information. In this section you can search the whole site for any keywords, or look through the very useful site map that simplifies everything for you.

OTHER FEATURES

Film Loads of resources for the world of film making. Includes News, Resources, Independent filmmaking and World filmmaking links.

Acting Those people who bring your writing to life, remember them? Well, they've got stacks of links to site of interest, too.

Reference Desk Everything you need for research and reference.

There's lots here, be patient, click lots of links and you'll find lots of good stuff.

www.scriptfactory.com
The Script Factory

Overall rating: ★★★★		
Classification: Official site	Content:	★★★★
Updating: Sporadically	Readability:	★★★
Navigation: ★★★★★	Speed:	★★★★★
UK		

'One of the leading centres for developing screenwriting talent', The Script Factory was founded in 1996, and as a result of their rehearsed readings of screenplays, many of those scripts have now been turned into films. They currently offer a selection of projects to help screenwriters develop their scripts. The site loads quickly from page to page but the design is a little pink. The links run down the left hand, pink column, and the content appears in the blue area. Many of the links appear as a PDF file, and you will need the Adobe Acrobat Reader to read it, which is readily available for free, elsewhere on the net.

SPECIAL FEATURES

What's On Details, prices and locations of the Events coming up that are sponsored by The Script Factory. Dates, details, prices, everything you need to know. At the time of writing, one such entry involved a showing of Bend It Like Beckham and a talk with the film's writers afterwards.

SCENE A programme of events that take place at film festivals. It's a new programme and they happily invite input for what the next SCENE might contain. The itinerary of previous events can be viewed by clicking the link.

Archives Prepare to be very impressed. Here you will find a huge list of the casting directors and actors who have taken part in the rehearsed readings of screenplays. It reads like a 'who's who' of the cream of British talent. Actors include, Helen Baxendale, Jim Broadbent, Tom Conti, Charles Dance, Christopher Eccleston, Dawn French, Nigel Havers, Geraldine James, Robert Lindsay, Neil Pearson, Stephen Rea and Joely Richardson.

Screen Writing Talent Details of the invaluable rehearsed readings of unproduced screenplays arranged by The Script Factory, and how to go about submitting your script.

Writers Passage Training A lottery funded project that supports new screenwriters. Nine feature film projects are taken through the initial stages of development. There are workshops with mentors and actors. All the details come as a PDF file.

Other Features They run a course for people who want to be the film company's first line of defence, the screenplay reader.

Excellent for screenwriters with finished scripts, wanting to get them developed. And for people wanting to be involved on the development side of filmmaking.

http://scriptwritingsecrets.com/
Scriptwriting Secrets

Overall rating: ★ ★ ★			
Classification:	Guide	**Content:**	★ ★ ★ ★
Updating:	Not	**Readability:**	★ ★ ★ ★ ★
Navigation:	★ ★ ★ ★ ★	**Speed:**	★ ★ ★ ★ ★

(US)

There are very few actual 'secrets' here. If there were, they would be for sale and every screenplay writer in the world would be queuing up to buy them. If you have wandered around the internet looking for help for writing screenplays, and more especially if you have looked at some of the other excellent sites in this chapter, you will see that everyone has their own ideas, their own advice, but ultimately it's very similar. This site, however, is not merely a list of articles, or links to other people's advice. This is a whole book, and it's free. To enter the site proper, click the Click Here To Begin button.

Once inside, you 'turn' the pages by clicking the blue links in the left column. You can work through them in order, or simply go to the chapter headings that are most useful to you. After each page of text, there are suggestions for where you might like to go next. Feel free to click away, everything loads quickly, use the back button on your browser to return to the previous page.

The beauty of this site is that it is a step by step guide. It's a conversational read and it covers the basics of putting your story down on the paper. It helps you not to make glaring mistakes with formatting and style. However, after a couple of pages you'll see why this book is free. It's a ploy to tell you how you can produce a workable script, but how, if you used Scriptware, (see entry in the For Sale section of this guide) you could get through the whole process more easily. And they're right, it would be easier, but don't worry, it's not essential. However, whether you decide to buy the software or not, this is a very useful site.

SPECIAL FEATURES

Reality Check Some basic guidelines about proper formatting and how to 'show' rather than 'tell'.

Formatting 101 This covers all the various elements of correct formatting. There's a Definition, a Description and examples, and how the use of Scriptware simplifies everything.

Intermediate Formatting Moving on from the formatting basics.

Advanced Formatting Many of these examples you would have to check the FAQ sections of other sites for. You may not need these all the time, but if you decide to use, say a phone call in your script, you would certainly question how to lay it down on paper. Question no more, it's all here.

Ready to Go? Once the script's finished, the hard work isn't over. Make sure whoever you send your work to gets it in the style and with the formatting they prefer. There are also printing considerations for you.

Scriptware If you've come this far, you may as well have a look at the one page honest-to-goodness advert for the software that's been plugged all the way through this site. You can even download a free demo.

As a step by step guide it's extremely helpful. It makes the software very tempting too.

www.writing.org.uk
Writing For Performance

Overall rating: ★ ★ ★ ★			
Classification:	Guide	**Content:**	★ ★ ★ ★
Updating:	Fortnightly	**Readability:**	★ ★ ★ ★ ★
Navigation:	★ ★ ★ ★ ★	**Speed:**	★ ★ ★ ★ ★

UK

Like much of the internet, many of the sites featured in this chapter are American. But it's not only the US that can produce sites overflowing with good advice, contacts and information. This British site proves the point.

As it's title suggests, this site has something for writers of any field of performed writing and you'll find this a helpful site whether you write, or want to write, for the television, radio, cinema or stage. However, the best section is the Television section. Occasionally, it becomes a portal site. It links you to the cream of a number of other sites, which appear without you actually leaving the Writing For Performance site. It's all simply designed, but attractive, which means that when you click the links down the right of every page, it loads fast, which we always approve of.

SPECIAL FEATURES

Television Robin Kelly, who runs the site, writes mostly situation comedy, so this section is exclusively dedicated to this especially tricky form of writing.

For starters, there's a complete guide to writing a situation comedy. Then there's a list of the top twenty places in Britain to send your completed script to. The Central Television Sitcom Workshop is a short page that describes, almost minute by minute what your episode should consist of, while Creating Comedy Characters speaks for itself. There are also a number of interviews with top writers of the genre, analysis of how the Americans create their situation comedies and a close look at the sitcom 'Friends'.

Film Small collection of links. David Zucker's 15 rules to writing comedy are a must. The Award Nominated Screenplays list Oscar nominees, but more importantly there are links to where the official books, and sometimes the scripts themselves, can be bought.

Radio There's an introduction to writing drama, information of what producers are looking for, which is essential if you are planning to sell your work and a guide to writing radio drama for the BBC, which is dated 1997, but is still relevant today.

Stage Read the lengthy book by Jerome K. Jerome, written in 1888 about the craft of writing dram for the stage. For a slightly more up to date view, Arnold Wesker's guide is there too.

Other Features There is a large collection of links under the Resources heading that include discussion lists, Industry News, places to pitch your work online and a list of templates that help you set out your writing properly.

You will also find a list of writing courses, recommended books. And various other more than useful links.

Excellent for the Situation Comedy writer but useful for writers of all performed writing.

OTHER SITES OF INTEREST

Coming Attractions
http://www.corona.bc.ca/films/

Basically, this site keeps you up to date with all the rumours and gossip surrounding yet-to-be-made films. The rumours turn into facts as the films go into production. Once made, all the information is still obtainable from the Archives which go back to 1995. This site is fascinating for writers because it shows you what's currently popular and what the industry is thinking of making in the future. You can search for films by genre, development stage or even name, if you know it. It also gives a frightening insight to how long an idea, then an optioned script, can be bounced around before anyone points a camera at it and shouts 'Action!'. If you're a screenwriter, this site will give you some idea of what you're up against.

The Horror Screenwriters Page
http://www.trenton.edu/~beres/horror.htm

If this is the genre that tickles your creative buds, then this isn't a bad place to find links in the field of horror. It's not pretty and simply runs and runs down the main page like a student being pursued through a forest by a axe-wielding maniac. So you want to write a horror screenplay, is simplistic in the extreme: '9. Write Your First Draft'. Better to read some of the sites, previously mentioned in this chapter, dedicated to the art of crafting a script. But, if horror is your thing, then there are dozens of gory links as well as ordinary writing links to interest you and help you on your way.

The Internet Movie Database
http://us.imdb.com/

It can't be said often enough, if you want to write films you need to know all about them, past and present. You need to be familiar with what's been made, what's popular etc. This is surely the biggest collection of movie information anywhere in the world? You'll find detailed information about 250,000 films and half a million people who were involved in making them. This is also a great resource for finding ideas for your own scripts. See what has been made and let the inspiration flow. Gigantic site.

The Movie Clichés List
http://www.moviecliches.com/

Very funny and very true. So many films feature the same ridiculous plots, character behaviour and coincidences. Non of them have any baring on our experiences in the real world. For example 'A villain will always commit murder right in front of the window when someone with binoculars is watching'. For writers, check your scripts and see how many of these stereotypical moments have crept in. If you can think of any more, they invite you to send them in.

whoRepresents?com
http://www.whorepresents.com/

Very basic site, but it provides a useful free service. Maybe you want to write something for a particular actor, and you want to get it to them directly. Sometimes finding an address can be difficult. This site lets you type in the name of an actor, and at the click of a button tells you who their American Agent, Attorney, Manager or Publicist are. You'll even find most of the representatives also have an address and phone number, so getting in contact couldn't be easier. Not every actor in existence is listed, but most are.

Chapter 09
verse

Originally this chapter was simply going to be called 'Poetry', but whilst researching a number of other sub-genres reared their heads: limericks and songwriting. So, although these only have one site each it seemed unfair to keep to the original title. Those two aside, what remains are some excellent poetry sites.

Poetry is one of the easiest forms of writing to undertake, and probably the easiest to do really badly. From student soul-searching to long rambling free-flowing verse, most of us have penned a poem at one time or another. Perhaps if we had perused these sites first we wouldn't be red faced at the thought of our less than perfect attempts.

Some sites are filled to overflowing with poems penned by famous published poets, where you can freely read how the professionals do it. Other sites concern themselves with personal poems and the giving and receiving of criticism, in order to improve. Some focus on the academic nature of poetry, its forms and terms.

Anyone can write a poem and whatever your standard or aspirations, these sites offer something for everyone.

www.poetrykit.org
The Poetry Kit

Overall rating: ★ ★ ★ ★ ★			
Classification:	Homepage	Content:	★ ★ ★ ★ ★
Updating:	Daily	Readability:	★ ★ ★ ★ ★
Navigation:	★ ★ ★ ★ ★	Speed:	★ ★ ★ ★ ★

UK

Simply designed UK site that provides links to other poetry related sites all over the world. It obviously started out as a much bigger project, containing articles, interview and individual poems. These three section still have interesting content but have nor been added to for some time. However, other parts of the site must keep the site owner busy around the clock. See below for details. All the links for the site can be found just under the site heading on the homepage, but the main, up to the minute sections are also available in the large box a little further down the page. The three red headings have lots of pages within them, click the blue links for more details. There is also a newsletter which is emailed free to subscribes on the first of every month.

SPECIAL FEATURES

Events Amazing collection of poetry happenings from all over the globe. Different sections cover, Africa, UK, Europe, USA and more. There are also pages carrying detail of mostly British Radio and TV programmes of interest. A handful of internet events are available too. Unlike so many other homepages on the internet, the details here are kept up to date, although a disclaimer says that responsibility is not taken for any inaccuracy. This is because much of the site details are sent in by the people who wish to advertise them. All will become clear once you get in and start browsing. You'll be surprised at just how much is going on.

Listings Includes a huge list of competitions, giving details of the prizes, the contact details and the entry fees. Includes one offs and on-going competitions. There is a list of interesting books and a far more impressive list of publishers world wide. The UK list alone has more than 100 entries. The courses section contains a wealth of information about both attendance and correspondence courses. There are also links to useful organisations, including poetry circles. The Who's Who section let's you write a short piece about yourself or read about the other poets who have passed through the site. Finally you are treated to links to individual poet's sites and a selection of workshop details from around the UK and abroad.

Magazines Contains a fantastic list of poetry and literary magazines. You will be amazed at how many UK ones there are. Most entries have details of how to contact the magazine and many also include subscription details. The online section is just about as comprehensive as you can find. There are other lists for Australia, Canada, India, Ireland, New Zealand and USA.

Other Features A handful of poems, articles and interviews. Great reading and a shame they are no longer being updated.

Want to know what's happening in poetry? On paper, in cyberspace, or even in the good old fashioned in the real world, it's all here.

www.poetrymagic.co.uk
Poetry Magic

Overall rating: ★★★★		
Classification: Guide	**Content:**	★★★★
Updating: Occasionally	**Readability:**	★★★★★
Navigation: ★★★★	**Speed:**	★★★★★

(UK)

It's unusual to find a site that has dedicated itself to 'the theory and craft of writing poetry'. At this site you'll find more than 100,000 words commenting on a range of issues, discussing what poetry is, why is it difficult to write and how does it differ from prose writing? Much of the information here is unique to the site and collected together by C. John Holcombe who for many years was Chairman of Phoenix Poets, as well as being widely published in UK small presses.

The site is easy to navigate and is organised into two sections, beginners and advanced. Links to both sections run down the left side of the site.

Poetry Magic is attractively designed. Much of it appears to have been produced on a top quality ivory coloured parchment paper, which is instantly more relaxing on the eyes than the usual stark white backgrounds we have come to expect from the majority of web pages.

It is worth mentioning that Poetry Magic lacks the 'chatty' tone of many writing sites, and although friendly it has an academic air. It is also obviously aimed at the slightly older audience by it's suggestion that people have more time to write poetry when they have retired or when the children have left home. That said, the information here is very useful whatever your age or experience.

SPECIAL FEATURES

Beginners A journey of poetic discovery starting with 'What is Poetry?' Step by step the reasons for writing are explored, followed by essays pondering various types of poetry, including modernist and experimental. Then there are a series of essays looking at the content of verse. Being original, themes, imagery and metaphor, rhythm and stanza are all discussed in detail. Finally there are excellent pages about the life of a poem once the writing is finished, covering critiquing, performance, publication, as well as ezines, books and magazines on poetry. Each section is presented in a similar vein: a fairly general point is stated, or a question asked, then the meat of the page is taken up with an intelligent discussion about it. There are also links to poetry online and more than 130 links to resources. There is also a long list of suggested books for you to read.

Advanced The darker stripes are the section headings, but you must click the lighter stripes underneath to access the information. Don't be put off by the fact that most of the lighter stripes simply say 'introduction'. There would be so many lines if everything were listed that this is purely an exercise in saving space. Once you've entered the Advanced section, all the essay heading appear on the left. The whole section takes the discussion way beyond the needs of the casual scribe, entering the realms of Hermeneutics, Jungian criticism and Chaos theory approaches to poetry. Heady stuff.

Professional For only five dollars you get 30 day access to this section, during which time you can download all the pages and read them at your leisure. It has 71 pages filled with almost 170,000 words. The full contents can be found by scrolling down the page. The fee can be paid securely online by credit card.

Intelligent, academic and fascinating site for poets.

www.poetrysociety.org.uk
The Poetry Society

Overall rating: ★★★★★			
Classification:	Official page	**Content:**	★★★★
Updating:	Frequently	**Readability:**	★★★★
Navigation:	★★★★★	**Speed:**	★★★★★

(UK)

The Society has more than 4000 members across the world. They produce publications, run Britain's longest running poetry competition, promote projects and are involved with educational work. Full UK membership will cost you £32 for the year.

The site is highly professional but fairly laid back and the simple design helps to keep the pages loading quickly to your browser . Everything you need is right there on the homepage, the different links have a brief description so you know exactly where you're wandering.

SPECIAL FEATURES

About Us Straightforward and informative page about the society and what they do.

Join Us Online! The various membership details are explained as are the benefits of joining. There are details of how you can join, both online and more traditionally, by post.

Events Links to what's going on including competitions, screenings, lectures and events taking place at the Poetry Café in Covent Garden.

The Poetry Shop Subscribe to their publications, join the Society, make donations. You can also purchase books, past issues of the Poetry review, and even copies of the posters used for Poetry on the Underground.

Poetry Review Both current and past issues of the magazine may be viewed and a selection of the articles, reviews and featured poems can be accessed for free. The entire copy can generally be purchased from the Poetry Shop section of the site.

Education Excellent page of resources for younger poets and for schools.

Other Features There is a whole site dedicated to teachers who 'want to bring poetry alive in the classroom'. Articles can be read from copies of the Poetry News. There is also an excellent page of permanent and Lively Links, which will be available for a shorter time. There is information about the National Poetry competition, past winners and how to enter this year.

Very informative website and with such reasonable membership rates the Society is a must for all poets.

www.poets-corner.org
Poet's corner

Overall rating: ★★★★★			
Classification: Library		**Content:**	★★★★★
Updating: Frequently		**Readability:**	★★★★★
Navigation: ★★★★★		**Speed:**	★★★★★

(US)

6,700 poems by 780 poets. Here simply so you can enjoy the poetry, and maybe learn a little something as a writer. Some very famous, some less so. All very pleasantly presented with alphabetical links to both the writers and their work, which makes for easy navigation. The site is nice and speedy and the design is attractive yet simple.

SPECIAL FEATURES

Author Index A quick find list for all the poets in the collection.

Title Index Alphabetical list of all the poems. Choose the first letter from the list at the top, the poems appear below.

Subject Index Looking for a particular theme or topic? This list of more than 50 subjects should help.

Bookshelf Currently there are 99 complete books encompassing Major Works, Collections and Anthologies.

Other Features FAQ and a detailed mission statement. A very necessary search engine. A handful of poets have brief biographies, however, soon every poet on the site will have one. Many of the poet have a photo, sketch or paining in the Faces of the Poets section. There is a whole section dedicated to Traditional Works from around the world.

Excellent resource and reminder to all poets of what can be achieved.

www.poettext.com/default.php
Poettext.com

Overall rating: ★★★★			
Classification: Portal		**Content:**	★★★★★
Updating: Constantly		**Readability:**	★★★★
Navigation: ★★★★		**Speed:**	★★★★

(UK)

This is a UK site for everyone who writes or reads poetry. There's a real notice-board feel to the homepage, with tasters of complete articles you can read by clicking the taster title. There's a leaning towards reading poetry, and then buying books from the online book shop. However, they make a good point that anyone who is serious about their poetry writing simply has to read poetry. So there. Sponsor adverts are dotted around the place too. You may have to get your browsing boots on to really get the most out of this site. The navigation links are in the top left hand corner, with recommended features further down in the same column.

SPECIAL FEATURES

Bookshop Really excellent selection of more than 4000 books. They miss the opportunity for impulse buying, by not tempting you with a range of books. They leave it up to you to browse for specifics in the search box at the top of the page. You can search by Title, Author, ISBN, or choose All for a less specific search. The server is completely secure when ordering online so you don't have to worry about the safety of your credit card details. Delivery times and availability are found under the book details. A very useful feature, Compare, is found just above the Add To Cart button. This shows you how much the title would cost you, including postage, if you bought it from a couple of rival bookshops, namely Amazon.co.uk. and BOL. Poettext was the cheapest in every comparison we looked at, which means you not only get great books, you get great bargains too.

Events Requires help from people around the country, sending details of their local events. Venues, descriptions, times and occasionally contact details are included with the listings. Some months have had more than 30 event listings each from around the UK.

Publications Lots of small press magazine. Details include their cost, contact details and payment details for publication in their pages.

Competitions Dozens of competitions and all the details you need to get involved. They are organised by month according to the submissions deadline. At the bottom of the month list is a page of on-going competitions. The Helpful Hints link talks you through how you might best make competitions work for you. It's the same page if you click the Tips For Wannabes in the links on the left.

Organisations Arts boards, appraisal services, writers' circles, libraries and more. Someone to contact about almost anything to do with poetry.

Highlighted Features Within this section poets can create their own portfolio and add their own work to the site. There are details of awards and prizes, the Editor's section, and various pages of information about performance poetry, articles on poets through history and a showcase of poetry by contemporary writers.

Other Features There's a news archive, poetry links, and a constant invitation to get involved by writing reviews and comments on what you find here.

Already one of the best UK poetry sites, if it continues to grow after its launch it may very well become the number one site.

---

www.poeticbyway.com/glossary.html
Bob's Byway – A Poetic Diversion

Overall rating: ★★★★			
Classification:	Homepage	**Content:**	★★★★
Updating:	Frequently	**Readability:**	★★★★★
Navigation:	★★★★★	**Speed:**	★★★★★

US

You can probably tell, by the title, that this is an honest-to-goodness homepage. Very often that means good intentions with mediocre results. Not in this case. This one is really good. That's why it's here. It has only a couple of features but they are explored in depth, on well designed, attractive pages that load surprisingly quickly. The first decision you have to make is whether to take the Direct or Scenic route to the good stuff. The scenic route is a wander through a few paragraphs which are little more than tenuous fronts for a selection of links to pages within the site. Nothing wrong with that and it serves as a distraction, but for the real meat of the site click the Direct Route link or any of the four links in the opening paragraph. You will get to the good stuff either way.

SPECIAL FEATURES

Glossary of Poetic Terms Enormous list of terms from 'ABCEDARIAN POEM' to 'Zeugma'. Each entry has a full definition and links to other words where necessary. You can browse through alphabetically, or have the whole A-Z on a really long page that, obviously, takes longer to load as it's 338K.

Examples of Poetic Terms Almost fifty different poets have their work on display which is used to highlight some of the poetic terms from the glossary. Now you not only know what they are called, but also how to recognise them.

Tips for the Enjoyment of Poetry Most people visiting the site probably won't need to be told how to enjoy poetry, but you never know.

Other Features Why not read some of Bob's poetry while you're here? You will also find Poetry, Literature and Reference links to other sites.

Useful site that explains many terms from simple to obscure.

http://kalliope.hypermart.net/			
Kalliope Poetics			
Overall rating: ★ ★ ★ ★			
Classification:	Online workshop	Content:	★ ★ ★ ★
Updating:		Readability:	★ ★ ★
Navigation:	★ ★ ★ ★	Speed:	★ ★ ★ ★ ★
US			

A flexible online workshop set up by poets who wanted to take part in something like this, but simply couldn't find it on the net. It is based on participants doing exercises They post their work, critique other people's and expect feedback for their own. You can join in by becoming an active member of one of the free online forums. Or, if you prefer, simply tackle the exercises on your own, in your own time and for your own benefit alone. As with all free workshops you will get out of it what you put in. There are no tough entry requirements here, no complex rules and regulations.

The design has had some thought, differing from the normal black type on white background usually found on websites. However, the background design, which works so well for the front page, actually hinders reading of further pages. The brown column on the left of the front page is where the site links live. This column, the brown one, on the front page is where the site links live. Click the colourful icons. You'll get the picture when you venture in. This is a very useful place for poets who want feedback, help or simply want to experiment with the exercises for their own private practice.

SPECIAL FEATURES

Introduction Not a feature as such, and the link is in the body of the front page rather than in the left hand column. However, this is essential reading before you go any further. This is where you'll find out what's going on and why.

To Join Details of the nine groups, how to join and what to expect.

Exercise Archive Whether you join the mailing list or not, you can access the exercises from here. They include basic and advanced exercises, so you can work at your own level and only on the ones that inspire you. There are warm up exercises, the basics are covered, as are various forms of poetry.

Other Features Links to online and print reference material.

Great exercises to get your poetry flowing.

---

www.poetryboard.com
PoetryBoard.com

Overall rating: ★★★★			
Classification: Forum		Content:	★★★★
Updating: Constantly		Readability:	★★★★★
Navigation: ★★★★★		Speed:	★★★★★

(UK)

Poetry people get together, swap ideas, help each other out, offer poems for others to read. The site was only set up in December 2000, but already it has amassed more than 2200 members and the postings to the various forums have already passed 100,000 posts! Which you have to agree is a lot, and both those numbers are rising all the time. The site is simple, but for the amount of traffic it's still a fast one. The homepage is like a master board. It lists the different forums available. For each forum you can see the number of threads, the number of posts and how recently someone posted to it. At the time of writing there were new post in every forum, within the last couple of hours, so none of the threads have much time to go stale. That's not to say that this site is so bursting with people and general activity that a visitor will feel swamped or feel that the site is verging on chaos. Everything is neat, tidy and in its place. And frankly, there tend to be a manageable number of people at the site at any one time. You can see exactly who is there by scrolling to the bottom on the homepage. Click on any individual person's name for their profile.

There are no features as such, just poets sharing their work, their thoughts and kindly critiquing each others poems. Individual forums include ones dedicated to Haiku, Short Compositions (which also includes short pieces of prose), and mystical thoughts. There are forums for specific genres of poetry including Dark, Love, Humour, Abstract and lyrical, which also includes song lyrics. There is also a Reviewers section were poems get the once over from other poets. Finally there's The Lounge, which is available for people to discuss anything they like, whether poetry related or not.

So many poets, so many poems, so little time.

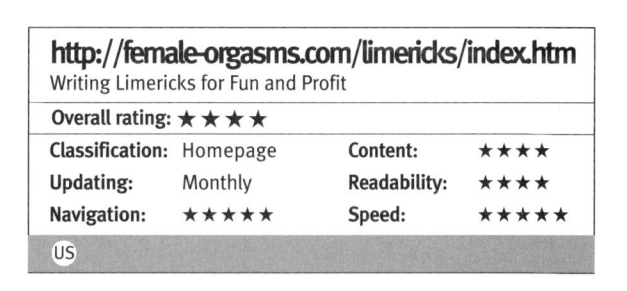

http://female-orgasms.com/limericks/index.htm
Writing Limericks for Fun and Profit

Overall rating: ★★★★			
Classification:	Homepage	**Content:**	★★★★
Updating:	Monthly	**Readability:**	★★★★
Navigation:	★★★★★	**Speed:**	★★★★★

US

Firstly, a note about the address of this site. The owner is a Sexologist and Sexuality Educator, and the limericks pages are only a smaller part of a site concerning his proper work. Hence the slightly headline grabbing address.

Limericks are possibly the easiest form of poetry to write. Purists might claim they are not even proper poetry, and much of the time they should probably be right. Even so, who knew there were so many rules about limericks that could be learnt? This site has them all. And lots of examples, many of them quite funny. The how-to tips run all the way down the homepage. You'll find onward links at the bottom.

SPECIAL FEATURES

A Dozen How-To Tips for Beginners Makes for interesting, if occasionally, unnecessary reading. Discusses the rhyme, metre and the form of limericks.

Additional Tips, Suggestions and Limericks More of the same, but the design is nicer. All new and original limericks for you to enjoy.

Other Features Fairly large collections of Bawdy and Clean limericks, depending on your preference. And only if it tickles your fancy, as it were, there's a link to the medically minded Female Orgasm pages.

Great to see that even skills for writing limericks can be learned.

OTHER SITES OF INTEREST

New Linked Poetry Forms for Sharing
http://www.into.demon.co.uk/newforms.htm

Simply put, this is a list of 42 new forms of poetry, most created by the same person. They can be written by one person or a collective. They all have their own rules and themes and examples are shown. If you want to try something new in poetry, this will have your creative juices flowing in no time. Strangely fascinating.

The Poetry School
http://www.bps.dircon.co.uk/html/poetry/poetsch.htm

Frankly uninspiring website that is little more than a page advert for the courses they run. However, these courses may be of rather more interest, especially to poets in the London area. There is a little background about the school and the tutors, who are all published poets. Tutorials, Seminars and Consultations are available at a variety of prices. There are even postal tutorials available for those unable to travel to London.

Songwriters Directory
http://www.songwritersdirectory.com/

Lyricists and their musical counterparts will find just about everything they want here. Resources will help you find associations, music industry news and more. Search the Songwriters Listings or even apply to have yourself put up there with your email address, photo and links to your sites. There is a small charge for the service. There is also a market place, a Bulletin Board for discussions, and lots more.

glossary of internet terms

A

Accelerators Add-on programs which speed up browsing.

Acceptable Use Policy These are the terms and conditions of using the internet. They are usually set by organisations who wish to regulate an individual's use of the internet. For example, an employer might issue a ruling on the type of email which can be sent from an office.

Access Provider A company which provides access to the internet, usually via a dial-up account. Many companies such as AOL and Dircon charge for this service, although there are an increasing number of free services such as Freeserve, Lineone and Tesco.net. Also known as an Internet Service Provider.

Account A user's internet connection, with an Access/Internet Service Provider, which usually has to be paid for.

Acrobat Reader Small, freely-available program, or web browser plug-in, which lets you view a Portable Document Format (PDF) file.

Across Lite Plug-in which allows you to complete crossword puzzles online.

Address Location name for email or internet site, which is the online equivalent of a postal address. It is usually composed of a unique series of words and punctuation, such as my.name@house.co.uk. See also URL.

America Online (AOL) The world's most heavily subscribed online service provider.

Animated GIF Low-grade animation technique used on websites.

ASCII Stands for American Standard Code for Information Interchange. It is a coding standard which all computers can recognise, and it ensures that if a character is entered on one part of the internet, the same character will be seen elsewhere.

ASCII Art Art made of letters and other symbols. Because it is made up of simple text, it can be recognised by different computers.

ASDL Stands for Asynchronous Digital Subscriber Line, which is a high speed copper wire allowing for rapid transfer of information. Not widely in use at the moment, but the government is pushing for its early introduction.

Attachment A file included with an email, which may be composed of text, graphics and sound. Attachments are encoded for transfer across the internet, and can be viewed in their original form by the recipient. An attachment is the equivalent of putting a photograph with a letter in the post.

B

Bookmark A function of the Netscape Navigator browser which allows you to save a link to your favourite sites, so that you can return directly to it later without re-entering the address. Favourites in Internet Explorer is the same thing.

BPS Abbreviation of Bits Per Second, which is a measure of the speed at which information is transferred or downloaded.

Broadband A type of data transfer medium (usually a cable or wire) which can carry several signals at the same time. Most existing data transfer media are narrowband and can only carry one signal at a time.

Browse The common term for looking around the web. See also Surfing.

Browser A generic term for the software that allows users to move and look around the web. Netscape Navigator and Internet Explorer are the ones that most people are familiar with, and they account for 97 per cent of web hits.

Bulletin Board Service A BBS is a computer with a telephone connection, which allows you direct contact to upload and download information and converse with other users via the computer. It was the forerunner to the online services and virtual communities of today.

C

Cache A temporary storage space on the hard drive of your computer, which stores downloaded websites. When you return to a website, information is retrieved from the cache and displayed much more rapidly. However, this information may not be the most recent version for sites which are frequently updated and you will need to reload the website address for these.

Chat Talking to other users on the web in real time, with typed instead of spoken words. Special software such as ICQ or MIRC is required before you can chat.

Chat Room An internet channel which allows several people to type in their messages and talk to one another over the internet.

Clickstream The trail left as you 'click' your way around the web.

Codec Any technology which can compress/decompress data, such as MPEG and MP3.

Content The material on a website that actually relates to the site, and is hopefully of interest or value. Things like adverts are not considered to be part of the content. The term is also used to refer to information on the internet that can be seen by users, as opposed to programming and other background information.

Cookie A cookie is a nugget of information sometimes sent by websites to your hard drive when you visit. They contain such details as what you looked at and what you ordered, and can add more information so the website can be customized to suit you.

Cybercafe Cafe where you use a computer terminal to browse the net for a small fee.

Cyberspace When first coined by the sci-fi author William Gibson, it meant a shared hallucination which occurred when people logged on to computer networks. It now refers to the virtual space you're in when you're on the internet.

D

Dial Up Refers to both a temporary telephone connection to your ISP's computer and how you make contact with your ISP each time you log onto the internet.

Domain The part of an internet address which identifies an individual computer. This can often be a business or person's name. For example, in the goodwebguide.com the domain name is theGoodWebGuide.

Download Transfer of information from an internet server to your computer.

Dynamic HTML The most recent version of the HTML standard.

E

Ecash Electronic cash which is used to make transactions on the internet.

Ecommerce The name for business which is carried out over the internet.

Email Mail which is delivered electronically over the internet. Usually comprised of text messages, but can contain illustrations, music and animations. Mail is sent to an email address, which is the internet equivalent of a postal address.

Encryption A process whereby information is scrambled to produce a 'coded message' which can't be read while in transit on the internet. The recipient must have decryption software in order to read the message.

Expire Term referring to newsgroup postings which are automatically deleted after a fixed period of time.

Ezine Publication on the web which is updated regularly.

FAQ Stands for frequently asked questions. This section can often be found on websites where the most common enquiries and their answers are archived.

Frame A method which splits web pages into windows.

F

FTP/File Transfer Protocol Standard method for transporting files across the internet.

G

GIF/Graphics Interchange Format A format in which graphics are compressed and a popular method of putting images on the internet, as they take little time to download.

Gopher The gopher was the precursor of the world wide web and consisted of archives accessed through a menu, usually organised by subject.

GUI/Graphical User Interface This is the system which turns binary information into the words and images format you can see on your computer screen. For example, instead of seeing the computer language which denotes the presence of your toolbar, you actually see a toolbar.

H

Hackers A term used to refer to expert programmers who used their skills to break into computer systems, just for the fun of it. Nowadays the word is more commonly associated with computer criminals, or Crackers.

Header Basic indication of what's in an email: who it's from, when it was sent and what it's about.

Hit When a file is downloaded from a website it is referred to as a 'hit'. Measuring the number of hits is a rough method of counting how many people visit a website. Not wholly accurate as one website can contain many files, so one visit may generate several hits.

Homepage Usually associated with a personal site, but it can also refer to the first page on your browser or the first page of a website.

Host Computer on which a website is stored. A host computer may store several websites, and usually has a fast, powerful connection to the internet. Also known as a Server.

HTML/Hypertext Mark-Up Language The computer code used to construct web pages.

HTTP/Hypertext Transfer Protocol The protocol for moving HTML files across the web.

Hyperlink A word or graphic which has been formatted so that you move from one area to another when you click on it. See also hypertext.

Hypertext Text within a document which is formatted so that it acts as a link from one page to another or from one document to another.

I

Image Map A graphic which contains hyperlinks.

Interface What you actually see on the computer screen.

Internet One or more computers connected to one another is an internet (lower case i). The Internet is the biggest of all the internets and consists of a worldwide collection of interconnected computer networks.

Internet Explorer One of the most popular pieces of browser software, produced by Microsoft.

Intranet A network of computers which works the same way as an internet but for internal use; such as within a corporation.

ISDN/Integrated Services Digital Network Digital telephone line which facilitates very fast connections and can transfer large amounts of data. It can carry more than one form of data at once.

ISP/Internet Service Provider See Access Provider.

J

Java Programming language which can be used to create interactive multimedia effects on web pages. It is used to create programmes known as applets, which add features such as animations, sound and even games to websites.

Javascript A scripting language which, like Java, can be used to add extra multimedia features. In contrast with Java, it does not consist of separate programmes. Javascript is embedded into the HTML text and can be interpreted by the browser, provided that the user has a Javascript enabled browser.

JPEG Stands for Joint Photographic Experts Group and is the name given to a type of format which compresses photos so that they can be seen on the web.

K

Kill file A function which allows a user to block incoming information from unwanted sources. Normally used on email and newsreaders.

LAN/Local Area Network A type of internet, but limited to a single area such as an office.

L

Login The account name or password needed to access a computer system.

Link Connection between web pages, or one web document and another, which are accessed via formatted text and graphic.

M

Mailing List A discussion group which is associated with a website. Participants send their emails to the site, and it is copied and sent by the server to other individuals on the mailing list.

Modem A device for converting digital data into analogue signals for transmission along standard phone lines. The usual way for home users to connect to the internet or log into their email accounts. May be internal (built into the computer) or external (a desk-top box connected to the computer).

MP3 A compressed music file format, which has almost no loss of quality although the compression rate may be very high.

N

Netscape Popular browser, now owned by AOL.

Newbie Term for someone new to the Internet. Used pejoratively about newcomers to bulletin boards or chat, who commit the sin of asking obvious questions or failing to observe the netiquette.

Newsgroup Discussion group amongst Internet users who share an interest. There are thousands of newsgroups covering every possible subject.

O

Offline Not connected to the internet via a telephone line.

Online Connected to the internet via a telephone line.

Offline Browsing A function of the browser software which allows the user to download pages and read them offline.

Online Service Provider Similar to an access provider but provides additional features such as live chat.

P

PDF/Portable Document Format A file format created by Adobe for offline reading of brochures, reports and other documents with complex graphic design, which can be read by anyone with Acrobat Reader.

Plug-in Piece of software which adds functions (such as playing music or video) to another, larger software program.

POP3/Post Office Protocol An email protocol that allows you to pick up your mail from any location on the web.

Portal A website which offers many services, such as search engines, email and chat rooms, to which people are likely to return to often. ISPs such as Yahoo and Alta Vista provide portal sites. These are the first thing you see when you log on and, in theory, act as gateways to the rest of the web.

Post/Posting Information sent to a usenet group, bulletin board, message board or by email.

PPP/Point to Point Protocol The agreed way of sending data over dial-up connections, so that the user's computer, the modem and the internet server can all recognise it. It is the protocol which allows you to get online.

Protocol Convention detailing a set of actions that computers in a network must follow so that they can understand one another.

Q

Query Request for specific information from a database.

R

RAM/Random Access Memory Your computer's short term memory.

Realplayer G2 A plug-in program that allows you to view video in real-time and listen to sound, and which is becoming increasingly important for web use.

Router A computer program which acts as an interface between two networks and decides how to route information.

S

Searchable Database A database on a website which allows the user to search for information, usually by keyword.

Search Engine Programs which enable web users to search for pages and sites using keywords. They are usually to be found on portal sites and browser homepages. Infoseek, Alta Vista and Lycos are some of the popular search engines.

Secure Transactions Information transfers which are encrypted so that only the sender and recipient have access to the uncoded message, so that the details within remain private. The term is most commonly used to refer to credit card transactions, although other information can be sent in a secure form.

Server A powerful computer that has a permanent fast connection to the internet. Such computers are usually owned by companies and act as host computers for websites.

Sign-on To connect to the internet and start using one of its facilities.

Shareware Software that doesn't have to be paid for, or test version of software that the user can access for free as a trial before buying it.

Skins Simple software that allows the user to change the appearance of an application.

Standard A style which the whole of the computer industry has agreed upon. Industry standards mean that hardware and software produced by the various different computer companies will work with one another.

Stream A technique for processing data, which enables it to be downloaded as a continuous stream, and viewed or listened to as the data arrives.

Surfing Slang for looking around the Internet, without any particular aim and following links from site to site.

T

TLA/Three Letter Acronyms Netspeak for the abbreviations of net jargon, such as BPS (Bits Per Second) and ISP (Internet Service Provider).

U

Upload To send files from your computer to another on the internet. When you send an email you are uploading a file.

URL/Uniform Resource Locator Jargon for an address on the internet, such as www.thegoodwebguide.co.uk.

Usenet A network of newsgroups which form a worldwide system on which anyone can post 'news'.

V

Virtual Community Name given to a congregation of regular mailing list/newsgroup users.

VRML/Virtual Reality Modeling Language Method for creating 3D environments on the web.

W

Wallpaper Description of the sometimes hectic background patterns which appear behind the text on some websites.

Web Based Email/Webmail Email accounts such as Hotmail and Rocketmail, which are accessed via an Internet browser rather than an email program such as Outlook Express. Webmail has to be typed while the user is online, but can be accessed from anywhere on the Web.

Webmaster A person responsible for a web server. May also be known as System Administrator.

Web Page Document which forms one part of a website (though some sites are a single page), usually formatted in HTML.

Web Ring Loose association of websites which are usually dedicated to the same subject and often contain links to one another.

Website A collection of related web pages which often belong to an individual or organisation and are about the same subject.

World Wide Web The part of the Internet which is easy to get around and see. The term is often mistakenly interchanged with Internet, though the two are not the same. If the Internet is a shopping mall, with shops, depots, and delivery bays, then the web is the actual shops which the customers see and use.

Index

AAA, see Association of Authors Agents
Absolute Write 20
abstract poetry 124
academic subjects, see education
accountancy, see legal issues
actors, see screenwriting
Adams, Douglas 91
Adler & Robin Books 45
Adler, Bill 45
Adobe Acrobat 14, 15, 40, 52, 55, 68, 105, 113
advertising, see copywriting
advice, see self-help
agents 15, 35, 38, 41, 44-48, 50, 67, 71, 94, 98, 100, 102, 110, 116
see also, marketing, publishing, screenwriting
aids to writing, see audio tapes, books, buying products to aid writing, CDs, downloads, DVDs, software, videos, etc.
Aladdin 108
Allen Poe, Edgar 91
All Experts 82
almanacs 90, 94
alterations, see publishing
amateurs, see beginners
Amazon 12, 26, 39, 42-44, 46, 49, 65, 72-74, 106, 121
ammunition, see firearms
amusement, see fun
anatomy 84
animation 110
anthologies, see poetry
antonyms 91
Antz 108
appraisal, see feedback, reviews
Aristophanes 84
Aristotle's Poetics 109

armour 86
articles, see journalism, magazines, self-help
Art of Writing, The 35
Arts boards 58, 122
Arts Council, the 58
Ask Oxford 93
assignments, see exercises
Association of Authors' Agents 50
attorneys 116
auctions 86
audio;
  books 21
  tapes 14, 15, 18, 64
Author.co.uk 21
Authorlink 38
authors 14, 20, 21, 24, 28, 30, 31, 33, 34, 38-41, 45, 47, 60, 71-73, 78, 80, 84
  poets 118, 121
autobiographies, see life writing
Awakenings 109
awards 71, 80, 110, 115, 122
  see also, funding your writing

Baby Namer 83
background, see research, settings
ballistics, see firearms
Barber, John F., Ph.D. 54
Bartleby.com 84
Baxendale, Helen 113
Bay, Michael 13
BBC, the 102, 111, 115
BBC 'The Writers' Room' 111
beasts, see mythical beasts
Becoming a Writer 39
beginners 29, 30, 41, 79, 80, 90, 96, 107, 111, 119, 125
Bend It Like Beckham 113
Beverley Hills Cop 109

Bible, the 84, 91
bibliography 94
Billy Elliot 111
biographies 85, 88, 94, 121
  see also, life writing
Birkbeck College, University of London 107
Black Lace 74
Black on White 22
block, see writer's block
Bob's Byway – A Poetic Diversion 122
body;
  armour 86
  in death investigation, see forensic investigation
BOL 121
Bond, Stephanie 73
Booklocker 40
books;
  for purchase 12, 14, 15, 18, 20, 25, 26, 31, 33, 38, 43, 44, 46, 49, 52, 57, 64, 65, 67, 71-75, 79, 86, 87, 93, 106, 115, 118-121
  proposals, see proposals
  signings 71
  see also, e-books
booksellers 71, 73
britannica.co.uk 94
Broadbent, Jim 113
broadcasting 68, 71, 111
  see also radio, screenwriting, television
Brooks, James L. 13
BUBL LINK 85
bullets, see firearms
business, see legal issues, marketing, publishing, screenwriting
searches, see directories
writing 33, 52, 90, 93

busy lives, see combining writing with other occupations
buying products to aid writing 12-18, 24-26, 28
  see also, audio tapes, books, CDs, DVDs, e-books, software, videos, etc.

calendar of events for specific years 72
Campaign Against Censorship of the Internet in Britain 61
cards, see greeting cards
careers in writing, see combining writing with other occupations, jobs
cassettes, see audio tapes
CDs 14, 21, 94
censorship 61
Central Television Sitcom Workshop, the 115
certificates 107
  see also, courses
chaos theory and poetry 119
characters 13, 22, 26, 30, 36, 55, 77, 83, 87, 93, 94, 96, 97, 101, 115, 116
Chartered Institute of Journalists, The 68
Cheat Sheets 80
children's writing 20, 21, 29, 35, 47, 76, 79
  poetry 120
Christian writing 48
Christie, Agatha 84
cinema, see films, screenwriting
CIoJ, see Chartered Institute of Journalists, The
circles, see writing groups
classes, see courses

136 thegoodwebguide.co.uk

classical mythology, see
  mythology
classified advertisements 23, 34,
  38
  see also, jobs
classroom, see education,
  schools
clichés 116
climate, see weather
clues, see forensic investigation
Coffeehouse for Writers 23
collective nouns 93
combining writing with other
  occupations 30, 32, 73, 75
comedy 73, 110, 111, 115
  poetry 124
comic books 20
Coming Attractions 116
communities, see writing groups
competitions 15, 23, 28-30, 33,
  36, 43, 44, 46, 47, 60, 75, 80, 91,
  93
  poetry 118, 120, 122
  screenwriting 100, 102, 103,
  108
computing;
  for writers 33, 46, 63, 90
  research 85
  writing 65
conferences 33
Confucius 84
Constitution, the U. S. 91
Contentious 53
contests, see competitions
Conti, Tom 113
contracts 22, 109
  see also, legal issues
conventions, see events
coping with rejection, see
  rejection
CopSeek.com 85
copyright 29, 35, 53, 58, 63
  see also, legal issues
Copyright Licensing Agency 58
Copyrightvault.com 53
copywriting 60

correspondence courses, see
  courses
courses 13, 15, 18, 21, 23-25, 27,
  29, 30, 34, 35, 52, 60-64, 71, 74,
  87, 97, 101-103, 106, 110, 113,
  115, 118, 123, 126
Covent Garden 120
coverage 102
Crafty Screenwriting 96
Create Your Screenplay 97
creative;
  arts 85
  writing, see crime, fiction,
  poetry, romance, etc.
cricket 93
crime and mystery 18, 35, 36, 80
Crime Scene Investigator 86
crime scenes, see forensic
  investigation
Crime Time 80
Crime Writers' Association 80
critiques, see feedback
Critters Workshop 70
crosswords, see fun
cultures 82, 85
currency converter 88
current affairs 90
customer support 13, 17

Dagger award 80
Dance, Charles 113
dark;
  fantasy, see horror
  poetry 124
Darwin, Charles, see Origin of the
  Species
daytime serials, see serials
Declaration of Independence, the
  U. S. 91
definitions 91
demographics, see statistics
demos, see downloads
derivations of words, see English
  language, the
design, see website design
diaries, see life writing

dictionaries 84, 85, 88, 90, 93,
  94
digests, see directories
digital video 112
directions, see maps
directories 68, 71, 80
diseases, see medicine
Disney, Walt 108
DIY 90
Doctor Who 91
documentaries 110
document presentation, see
  formatting
Done Deal 12, 98
downloads 13-18, 24, 26, 40, 52,
  55, 67, 68, 77, 79, 99, 102, 114
drafts, see managing manuscripts
  or scripts
drama, see plays, radio,
  screenwriting, television
Drew's Script-O-Rama 99
Dr John's Eazy-Peazy Guide to
  Creative Writing Ideas 54
DV, see digital video
DVDs 94

e-books 14, 20, 21, 24, 28, 33,
  40, 67, 75, 79, 96, 105, 114
  see also, e-publishing
Eccleston, Christopher 113
e-commerce, see buying products
  to aid writing
editing, see publishing
education 85, 120
  see also, courses
electronic rights, see legal issues
Elements of Style, the 84
Elliot, T. S. 84
Elliott, Ted 108
e-mails, see e-books, newsletters,
  writing groups
Emma Holly ñ Erotica & Romance
  74
employment, see jobs
Encyclopaedia Britannica 94
Encyclopaedia Mythica, the 94

encyclopaedias 90, 94
  of legal terms 52, 90
  of old diseases 72, 90
  of poetic terms 122
  of writing 44
engineering, see technical
  writing
English language, the 23, 35, 52,
  58, 80, 84, 85, 91, 93
entertainment;
  amusement, see fun
  writing 61
e-publishing 48, 72, 77, 94
erotica 20, 74, 75
errors in writing, see English
  language, the
essays 36, 54, 57, 68, 84, 119
  see also, non-fiction, prose
events 79, 80, 107, 113, 118, 120,
  122
  see also, calendar
evidence, see forensic
  investigation
eWriteLife 24
exercises 23, 24, 26, 27, 31, 35,
  54, 57, 62, 123, 124
  see also, courses
experts 82, 98, 110
e-zines 18, 20, 21, 26, 28, 32, 34,
  42, 46, 47, 55, 61, 71, 79, 80,
  103, 119

fantasy 29, 48, 70
farmers 90
fashion 72, 82
FBI, the 94
feature films, see films
feedback 23, 25-27, 30, 32, 34,
  41, 49, 60, 68, 70, 71, 77, 78
  on poetry 119, 122-124
  on scripts 97, 102-104, 110, 112
  see also, reviews
fees, see payment
fellowships, see funding your
  writing
festivals, see films

thegoodwebguide.co.uk 137

fiction 15, 18, 20, 24-26, 39, 42, 55, 69-80, 84, 85, 87, 90, 92, 94
see also, children's writing, crime, fantasy, romance, science fiction, short stories, etc.
Field, Syd 13, 106
films 82, 92, 97, 102, 106, 110-113, 115, 116
see also, screenwriting
Final Draft 13, 15
final polish, see managing manuscripts or scripts
finance, see business writing, payment
fingerprints, see forensic Investigation
firearms and weapons 86, 92, 94
FirearmsID.com 92
first draft, see managing manuscripts or scripts
first names, see characters
fitting writing in, see combining writing with other occupations
flash fiction 25, 55
Fly, The 109
folklore 94
foreign languages 29, 88
forensic investigation 86, 94
Forensic Science Resources 94
formatting 13-17, 21, 27, 41, 43, 52, 58, 64, 96, 97, 101, 111, 114
Freelance Writing 60
freelancing 14, 20, 28, 29, 60, 65
Freelancing 4 Money 60
French, Dawn 113
Friends 115
fun 20, 46, 54-56, 73, 78, 88, 90, 91, 93, 102, 112, 116
funding your writing 58, 110, 120, 122
see also, payment
Funds for Writers 58
Furious Pen 55

games 82
Garbl's Fat-Free-Writing Links 58
genres, see fiction, screenwriting
Get Into It 57
gifts, see merchandise
glossary, see encyclopaedias
Godzilla 108
Google 90
Gorman, Ed 80
government bodies 63
grammar, see English language, the
grants, see funding your writing
Gray's Anatomy of the Human Body 84
greeting cards 29, 33, 44, 47, 58
groups, see writing groups
guidelines, see self-help
guides, see buying products to aid writing, courses, self-help
guns, see firearms

Haiku 99, 124
Hall, Lee 111
Hanks, Tom 13
Havers, Nigel 113
health, see business writing, medicine
help, see self-help
helplines, see customer support
hermeneutics 119
historical romances 72
Holcombe, C. John 119
Holly, Emma 73
Hollywood, see films, screenwriting
homework 90
see also, exercises
home writing, see combining writing with other occupations
homophones 91
horoscopes 90
horror 29, 70, 71, 116
Horror Screenwriters' Page, The 116
Horror Writers' Association 71
horses, see police
How Stuff Works 87
How to Get Paid Writing Simple Greeting Cards 58
humanities 85
humour, see comedy

ideas, see exercises, inspiration
illustrators 76
imagery 119
independent films, see films
indexing 35
industry 82
see also technical writing
Info Please 94
Inscriptions 46
Insider Guides 67
inspiration 54, 55, 57, 66, 87, 89, 90, 94, 101, 116
see also, exercises, writer's block
Inspired2write.com 27
intellectual property 50
see also, legal issues
interaction between writers, see feedback, writing groups
interactive stories 78
international rights 29
Internet, the 61, 90, 103, 118
see also, website design and setup
Internet Movie Database, The 116
Internet Writing Journal 33
Internet Writing Workshop 25
interviews, see authors, screenwriting
investigation, see forensic investigation
ISBN 72, 121
IT, see computing
iTools 88
IWJ, The, see Internet Writing Journal

James, Geraldine 113
jargon 93, 98, 105
Jerome, Jerome K. 115
jobs 28, 30, 33, 34, 38, 46, 47, 49, 60, 61, 79, 87, 110
journalism 32, 33, 35, 61, 63, 66, 68
Journalism UK 61
Journalist Express 68
journals, see life writing, magazines
Jungian criticism 119

Kalliope Poetics 123
Katy Terrega 75
Kelly, Robin 115
knives, see firearms and weapons
Koontz, Dean 71

language, see English language, the, foreign languages
law 88
see also, business writing, encyclopaedias, legal issues
layout, see formatting
lectures, see courses, events
legal issues 14, 29, 30, 35, 47-50, 53, 54, 60, 63, 76, 90, 94
letters, see business writing, life writing
libel, see legal issues
libraries, see research
life;
  sciences 85
  writing 14, 62, 84, 85, 88
limericks 91, 125
Lindsay, Robert 113
literary;
  agents, see agents
  websites 21
Literary Liaisons 72
literature, see fiction, non-fiction
Little Magazines 42
log line, see managing manuscripts or scripts
love;
  poetry 124
  stories, see romance
lyricists, see song writing

138 thegoodwebguide.co.uk

Mad Screenwriter 112
Mafia, the 94
magazines 14, 15, 21, 28, 33, 35, 41-44, 52, 60, 61, 64, 68, 71, 80, 89, 102, 110, 118-120, 122
see also, journalism
Maher, Chrissie 52
mailing lists, see newsletters
managers, see agents
managing manuscripts or scripts 24, 26, 44, 98, 105
manuscripts, see formatting, managing, marketing
maps 77, 88
marketing 13-15, 18, 20-22, 24, 28-30, 34, 35, 38, 43-48, 60, 64-67, 70, 73, 75, 80, 97, 98, 103, 105, 114
see also, agents, publishing, screenwriting
Mask of Zorro, The 108
Master Freelancer 14
mathematics 85
McCammon, Robert 71
medicine 72, 84, 85, 90, 94
merchandise 20, 30, 36
metaphor, see imagery
metre, see rhythm
military 90
Miss Piggy 91
misuse of language, see English language, the
mobile phones 93
Momwriters 30
moon phases 90
motion picture industry, see screenwriting
Movie Bytes 100
Movie Clichés List, The 116
movies, see films, screenwriting
music industry, see song writing
mystery, see crime and mystery
Mystery Vault.net 80
Mystery Writers' Forum 94
Mystery Writers' Resources 94
mystical thoughts 124

mythical beasts 94
mythology 84, 94

names, see characters
namingbaby.co.uk 83
National Poetry Competition 120
National Union of Journalists 63
networking, see feedback
New Linked Poetry Forms for Sharing 126
news 90
newsletters 13, 14, 20, 23, 26, 27, 33, 34, 39, 43, 44, 49, 53, 56, 58, 60, 62, 64, 65, 71, 72, 75, 80, 82, 86, 100, 108
newspapers, see journalism
new writers, see beginners
New Writers' Network, The 41
NiceStories.com 75
non-fiction 20, 22, 24-26, 41, 66, 68, 72, 80, 84, 90, 94
Non-Fiction Writers' Workshop, The 68
novels, see fiction
NUJ, see National Union of Journalists
nursery rhymes 91

one-liners 20
One of Us 31
online;
 learning, see courses
 publications, see e-books, e-zines
option agreements, see managing manuscripts or scripts
Origin of the Species, the 84
origin of words, see English language, the
Oscars, see awards
outline, see managing manuscripts or scripts
OWLS, see Oxford Word and Language Service
Oxford Shakespeare, the 84
Oxford University Press 93

Oxford Word and Language Service 93

papers, see life writing, newspapers, non-fiction
Paradise 58
payment 30, 49
 see also, funding your writing
Pearson, Barry 97
Pearson, Neil 113
pen friends 30
pensions, see business writing
people searches, see directories
performance, see plays, radio, screenwriting, television
poetry 119, 122
periodicals, see magazines
personal advertisements, see classified advertisements
pets 82
Philp, Tim 22
Phobia List, The 94
phobias 94
Phoenix Poets 119
photographs 77, 86, 90, 94, 121
physical sciences, see science
pictures, see illustrators, photographs
pitching, see marketing
plagiarism, see legal issues
Plain English 52
planning 22
plays 20, 49, 60, 80, 101, 110, 115
Playwriting Seminars, The 101
plots 13, 14, 16, 17, 22, 73, 80, 87, 101, 109, 116
 see also, inspiration
POD, see Print on Demand books
poetry 20, 23, 25, 29, 33, 35, 36, 48, 56, 84, 91, 99, 109, 117-126
PoetryBoard.com 124
Poetry Café, the 120
Poetry Kit, The 118
Poetry Magic 119

Poetry News, The 120
Poetry on the Underground 120
Poetry Review, The 120
Poetry School, The 126
Poetry Society, The 120
Poet's Corner 121
Poettext.com 121
poisons 94
police 85, 86, 94
politics, see government bodies, journalism
polls 99, 103
Polti's 36 Dramatic Situations 80
porn, see erotica
presentation, see formatting
presses, see publishing
Print on Demand books 40, 46
prizes, see awards
production, see plays, radio, screenwriting, television
products to aid writing, see books, buying products to aid writing, downloads, software
professional writing, see jobs
promotion, see marketing
proposals 46, 67
 see also marketing
prose 36, 69-80, 119, 124
 see also, fiction
protecting your writing, see copyright, legal issues, security
publications, see journalism, magazines
publicists, see agents
publicity, see marketing
Published! How to Reach Writing Success 64
Published Writer, The 47
publishing 21, 22, 28, 29, 32, 33, 35, 37-50, 56, 60, 61, 64, 66, 67, 71-73, 76, 77, 80, 89, 94, 118, 119
 see also, legal issues, marketing
Pub List 89
purchasing, see buying products to aid writing

thegoodwebguide.co.uk 139

Purple Crayon, The 76

qualifications 107
  see also, courses
query letters, see managing manuscripts or scripts
questions and answers 82, 87, 98, 106, 109-111
quizzes, see competitions
quotations 54, 84, 91, 93, 94, 101, 112

radio 49, 110, 111, 115, 118
  see also, broadcasting
Rea, Stephen 113
readers of manuscripts, scripts or screenplays 21, 38, 104, 111, 113
readings of scripts and screenplays 111, 113
reconstructions, see forensic investigation
Refdesk.com 90
reference, see research
registering scripts 13
rejection 47, 56
Rejection Collection.com 56
release forms, see managing manuscripts or scripts
reports, see business writing, feedback
reprints 29
Reproduction Rights Organisation 58
  see also, copyright
research 23, 24, 34, 46, 60, 63, 64, 68, 70-72, 76, 77, 81-94, 102, 112, 122, 123
  see also, almanacs, dictionaries, encyclopaedias, thesauri, etc.
resources, see buying products to aid writing, downloads, research, self-help
reviews of books, poetry, scripts, software, etc. 12, 16, 20, 21, 26, 28, 33, 36, 39, 46, 76, 80,103, 104, 110, 122, 124

  see also, feedback
revisions, see managing manuscripts or scripts
rhymes 88, 91
  see also, poetry
RhymeZone.com 91
rhythm 119, 125
Richardson, Joely 113
rights, see copyright, legal issues
Robin's Nest 35
Roget's Thesauri 84
romance 18, 25, 29, 35, 48, 72-74, 77, 80, 124
Romance Central 77
Rossio, Terry 108

Sassoon, Siegfried 84
Sayings of Confucius, the 84
Sayle, Alexei 91
scene reconstruction, see forensic investigation
schools, see courses, education
poetry in the classroom 120
science 85, 94
  fiction 29, 70
  writing, see technical writing
Scrabble 88
screenings of screenplays 111
screenplays, see screenwriting
Screenwriters' Cyberia 102
Screenwriters' Store 13, 15, 16
Screenwriters' Utopia, The 103
screenwriting 13-18, 20, 25, 33, 35, 44, 49, 60, 71, 80, 87, 95-116
  interviews with professionals 98, 106, 109-113, 116
  see also, competitions, marketing
Script Factory, The 113
Scriptorium, The 26
scripts, see plays, screenwriting
Script Shop 104
Scriptware 16, 114
Scriptwriters' Niche, The 105
Scriptwriting Secrets 114
Scriptwriting Success 105

search engines 77, 84, 90, 121
security 94
  see also, copyright
self-help 12-18, 20-36, 39, 43-46, 54, 55, 63, 65, 70-80, 86, 97, 103, 111, 112
  see also, buying products to aid writing, courses
self-publishing 32, 40
selling your manuscript or script, see marketing
seminars, see courses
serials 110
settings 22, 26, 72, 101
Shakespeare, William 84, 91
shopping, see books, buying products to aid writing
short stories 20, 35, 42, 75, 78
Shrek 108
situation comedy 115
skills, see self-help
small ads, see classified advertisements
social sciences 85
Society of Authors, The 35
software 12-18, 20, 24, 26, 31, 33, 62, 94, 102, 114
  see also, buying products to aid writing
Songwriters' Directory 126
song writing 32, 33, 53, 91, 124, 126
Sophocles 17
spelling, see English language, the
sport 61, 90, 93, 94
stage, see plays
stanza 119
starting out, see beginners
statistics 68
Stephanie Bond How-To Articles 73
step outlines, see managing manuscripts or scripts
stock market, see business writing

Stoker Awards 71
Stone, Oliver 13
stories, see fiction
Stories.com 78
structure of scripts 97, 101
studios, see films, screenwriting
study, see courses
style, see English language, the, fashion, formatting
submitting manuscripts, see agents, formatting, managing manuscripts or scripts, marketing, publishing
support, see customer support
suspense and thrillers 13
  see also, horror
Sydfield.com 106
synonyms 88, 91
  see also, thesauri

tapes, see audio tapes
tax, see legal issues
technical writing 20, 48, 60, 61, 85, 88
technology, see technical writing
teenage writing 25, 75
television 97, 99, 100, 110-112, 115, 118
  see also, broadcasting, screenwriting
terms, see encyclopaedias
Terrega, Katy 75
text messaging 93
theatre, see plays
themes 22, 101, 119
thesauri 84, 88, 93, 94
thrillers, see suspense and thrillers
tips, see self-help
titles 26
  see also, books
trademarks 88
training, see courses
transcripts 99
translations 29, 88
travel writing 65

140 thegoodwebguide.co.uk

treatments, see managing manuscripts or scripts
tuition, see courses

Underdown, Harold D. 76
universities 21, 107
University of London 107
updates, see newsletters
usage, see English language, the
U. S., the, see Constitution, Declaration of Independence
Utter Drivel 52

verse, see poetry
videos 13, 14, 72, 106, 111
Virgil 84
Virtual Script Workshop 107
voice, see plays

Wake Up Writing 31
Wald, Catherine 56
weapons, see firearms
weather 90, 94
webrings 33
website design and setup 20, 21, 41, 52, 53, 64, 88
Wehner, Chris 103
Wesker, Arnold 115
whoRepresents?.com 116
WIPO, see World Intellectual Property Organisation
women screenwriters 112
Wordplay 108
words, see English language, the
Wordweave 27
workshops, see courses
World Fact Book, the 84
World Intellectual Property Organisation 50
Worldwide Freelance Writers 65
Write4Kids.com 79
Writernet 109
writers, see authors
writerís block 22, 31, 54, 55, 57, 101
see also, exercises, inspiration

Writers' Cramp 36
Writers' Digest 43
Writers' Exchange 28
Writers' Guild of America Mentors 110
Writers' Guild of Great Britain 49
Writers' Handbook, The 49
Writers' Home, The 66
Writers' Manual 32
Writers' Market.com 44
Writers' Net 48
Writers' Resource Centre 36
Writers' Store, The 18
Writers Write 33
Writing For Performance 115
writing from home, see home writing
writing groups 21, 23-25, 27, 31, 33, 34, 41, 42, 49, 70
poetry 118, 122
Writing Limericks for Fun and Profit 125
Writing the Journey – Online Journal Writing Workshop 62
Writing World 29

Xrefer 94

Yahoo! Groups 34
You Can Write 67
young;
    adults, see teenage writing
    writers 26, 120
Yudkin, Marcia 64

Zappa, Frank 91
Zucker, David 115
Zwart, Elizabeth Clarkson 91

other great titles in thegoodwebguide series:

hardback   £12.99

antiques and collectables .... ISBN 1-903282-21-7
health .... ISBN 1-903282-08-x
home and interiors .... ISBN 1-903282-15-2
money .... ISBN 1-903282-26-8
museums and galleries .... ISBN 1-903282-14-4
travel .... ISBN 1-903282-05-5
wine .... ISBN 1-903282-04-7
world religions .... ISBN 1-903282-25-x

paperback   £7.99/£8.99

food .... ISBN 1-903282-17-9
gardening .... ISBN 1-903282-16-0
parents .... ISBN 1-903282-19-5
genealogy .... ISBN 1-903282-45-4

small paperbacks   £4.99

comedy .... ISBN 1-903282-20-9
games .... ISBN 1-903282-10-1
gay life .... ISBN 1-903282-13-6
music .... ISBN 1-903282-11-x
sex .... ISBN 1-903282-09-8
sport .... ISBN 1-903282-07-1
tv .... ISBN 1-903282-12-8